THE 10 WORST SERIAL KILLERS

THE 10 WORST SERIAL KILLERS

MONSTERS WHOSE CRIMES SHOCKED THE WORLD

VICTOR MCQUEEN

ARCTURUS

Picture Credits

Getty: 12 (Alejandra Matiz/Leo Matiz Foundation Mexico); 54 (Ullstein Bild); 68 (Jiji Press); 94 (Jeff Vinnick); 115 (Georges DeKeerie); 123 (Terry Fincher/Stringer); 130 (Hulton-Deutsch Collection); 154 (Bettmann); 158 (Bettmann); 161 (Bettmann); 180 (Sygma/Kapoor Baldev)

Associated Press: 17

Public domain: 140, 172

Rex: 91 (Canadian Press)

Shutterstock: 43 (HitManSnr/Shutterstock.com)

Topfoto: 58 (Ullstein Bild); 107

WA News: 41

ARCTURUS

This edition published in 2017 by Arcturus Publishing Limited
26/27 Bickels Yard, 151–153 Bermondsey Street,
London SE1 3HA

978-1-78599-380-0
DA004674UK

Printed in China

Contents

Introduction

Serial killers horrify and intrigue us in equal measure. Thankfully they are rare, accounting for less than 1 per cent of all murders committed worldwide each year. Yet we will never, it seems, be entirely free of them: they have stalked human society for hundreds of years, and each new generation produces a fresh crop of such predators, more cunning and deadly than the last.

The FBI defines serial murder as 'the unlawful killing of two or more victims by the same offender(s) in separate events'. The latter part of the definition is important, and is what distinguishes the serial killer from 'spree killers', such as school shooters. Although only two murders are technically required for a killer to be considered a 'serial killer', in reality most go on to kill several victims in separate events, and it is these offenders that we most closely associate with the term 'serial killer'.

This book looks at ten of the world's very worst serial killers. They have been selected not simply because of their high 'body counts': these killers are the ones who have most terrified the communities on which they preyed, and in some cases changed the history of the nations in which they operated. A particular killer, operating at a particular time in a particular country can commit crimes that reverberate throughout history and become part of a society's collective consciousness. As this book will demonstrate, serial killers operate in almost every continent on earth. Many myths and falsehoods have sprung up around such individuals, and their crimes have inspired countless sensationalist films, books and television series. This collection focuses solely on the true stories behind the very worst real-life serial killers from across the globe.

The truth, as we shall see, is far more terrifying than fiction.

CHAPTER ONE

Luis Alfredo Garavito Cubillos, 'The Beast'

In a lonely conifer forest on the outskirts of Villavicencio, 70 kilometres (43 miles) south-east of Bogotá, two boys ran for their lives. One was a 16-year-old, who had come to the forest in order to smoke marijuana; the other was 12-year-old John Ivan Sabogal, who had been taken to the forest at knifepoint, stripped and tied up. When his abductor pulled out a knife, John Ivan Sabogal had screamed for help, attracting the attention of the pot-smoking teenager. He found the young boy lying at the feet of a naked man and hurled abuse and then stones at the man. In panic, the man cut John Ivan's bonds and ordered him to run deeper into the forest. But the boy ran instead towards his rescuer, and the houses of Villavicencio. His furious attacker pursued both the boys through the forest and across a bridge over a creek, knife in hand. His name was Luis Alfredo Garavito Cubillos; he was the most prolific serial killer the world has ever known.

The boys reached a farm, where a six-year-old girl was playing in the fading light of the April evening. They hid, and when the killer arrived the girl pointed him in the wrong direction. The boys escaped and alerted the police, who immediately swarmed to the scene. Just a few months earlier they had found the bodies of 12 children close by. A mob of outraged locals soon joined the frantic hunt, creating chaos and confusion as to who were the hunters and who was the quarry. Night began to fall, with no sign of the killer. Corporal Pedro Babativa ordered the furious locals to return to their homes and, eventually – showering the police with abuse – they complied.

Soon after, from his hiding place deep in the woods, Luis Alfredo Garavito watched the headlights of the last police patrol car sweep across the dark road back towards Villavicencio. He brushed himself down and stepped out from the trees.

Others have claimed or been suspected of more murders, but in terms of proven victims, Luis Alfredo Garavito is the worst serial killer in history. He was found guilty of 138 murders between 1992 and 1999, and it is feared he may have killed as many as 400. Fellow-countryman Pedro Alonso López is his main challenger for the title of 'worst of the worst' with 110 confirmed murders and the suspicion he killed hundreds more. The world's third-worst serial killer, Daniel Camargo Barbosa, who killed at least 72 children, was also born in Colombia.

What is it about Colombia that has produced three such prolific serial killers? To answer that question, it is necessary to look at the long and bloody history of the country into which they were born.

The story of modern Colombia begins, predictably, with a murder.

The child of 'La Violencia'

In 1948, popular Liberal Party presidential candidate Jorge Eliécer Gaitán was assassinated, allegedly by a lone, deranged gunman called Juan Roa Sierra. Because the killer was murdered by an enraged mob before he could be brought to trial, Gaitán's assassination has been the subject of the same sort of conspiracy theories that swirl around US President John F. Kennedy's death at the hands of Lee Harvey Oswald (later killed by Jack Ruby). Battles between Liberal Party and Conservative Party supporters in the capital Bogotá soon spread to the rest of Colombia, engulfing the country in ten years of bloody conflict known as 'La Violencia'. As many as 200,000 people died. Conservative paramilitaries attacked peasant farms and schools, raping, killing and dismembering the children in order to terrorize their enemy into submission. They specialized in the 'neck-tie cut' – slitting a victim's throat and pulling his tongue out through the gaping wound.

It was during this period, on 25 January 1957, that Luis Alfredo Garavito was born, in one of the areas worst affected by the violence: Génova, Quindío. Génova is a small town surrounded by hills on the banks of the San Juan River. It lies in the central-west area of Colombia, a country whose borders include the South American countries of Venezuela, Ecuador, Peru and Brazil and the Central American country of Panama. Opposite Colombia's northern shore lies Cuba and the United States of America. Both have played a pivotal role in Colombia's bloody modern history.

Garavito was the oldest of seven brothers, and in testimony to investigators he claimed he was the victim of sexual abuse by two different neighbours, first when he was

The 'Bogotazo' riots, in 1948, Bogotá, Colombia. The bloody conflict between the Liberal and Conservative parties during 'La Violencia' claimed as many as 200,000 lives.

12 and then again when he was 15. At the time he was too afraid to tell anyone, least of all his father, who was also physically and mentally abusive towards him and his mother. Colombia has an aggressively macho culture, with domestic abuse and sexual violence being commonplace. Luis, the oldest child, later described his futile attempts to protect his mother from his father's beatings. The sound of her screams and the sight of her blood would stay with him throughout his life. His father was also strict about not allowing him girlfriends, further isolating the already painfully shy boy.

Beyond this, we can surmise that his family was typical of that area: peasant farmers, manual labourers or shopkeepers providing the basic necessities of life; one way or another, the Garavito family would have faced the same grinding poverty that was the lot of all but the landowning class in Génova. The area is now dominated by coffee plantations, but this was a novel crop in Colombia when Garavito was growing up: the staple Colombian crop prior to coffee was bananas. The same Andean mountain slopes produce high-quality coca leaves, which in the 1990s would attract the attention of Colombia's drug cartels, but in the 1960s the market for cocaine was relatively small.

Throughout the early 1960s, government-backed paramilitary attacks increased in frequency and violence. If Garavito did not witness at first hand the brutal murder and torture that these armed groups dispensed, it is almost certain he heard about it from his school friends and family. One of the most significant figures in Colombia's modern history was born in the same small town as Garavito, and it's impossible to imagine that he was not the talk of the school playground – a local hero, even.

Pedro Antonio Marín, known to the world as Marulanda, leader of the notorious Revolutionary Armed Forces of Colombia ('Fuerzas Armadas Revolucionarias de Colombia' or FARC) would take up arms against his government when Garavito was seven years old. That decision would be a fateful one, not just for Marín himself, but also for the entire country. To date, nearly a quarter of a million people have died during the long war between the guerillas, paramilitaries, drug cartels and government, and many thousands more have disappeared without a trace. Garavito's family was soon forced to flee their home, like 5 million other Colombians to date. They moved further west, to the village of Ceylon, near Trujillo, Valle del Cauca.

Garavito the outsider

The young Luis attended the local Simón Bolívar school until he was 16. Teachers found him to be withdrawn and distant, but by no means unintelligent. He was prone to violent temper tantrums, which he later put down to some underlying 'frustrations' at his own inability to be a better person. Discipline in Colombian schools was strict at this time, with most teachers carrying canes and belts, so it is almost certain that Luis was beaten for his poor conduct. Classmates bullied him and mocked the bespectacled, meek outsider. The country was then, and remains today, fervently Roman Catholic, and we know that his religious upbringing made a profound and lasting impression on Garavito.

From his early teens onwards, Garavito began to feel sexual attraction towards younger boys. His first sexual crimes were against his own brothers, whom he fondled as they slept. Then, whilst still a teenager, he attempted to lure a young boy away from the local train station. The boy started screaming when Garavito began to molest him, and Garavito was arrested by the local police. In response, his father threw him out of the family home.

Garavito found work initially on a local farm, then drifted through a series of low-end jobs, often in warehouses in and around his home town. He became an alcoholic early in life, and it is possible he was already consuming home-brewed alcohol, such as *guarapo* (from sugar-cane) or *chicha* (from maize), in childhood, a common phenomenon in rural parts of Colombia. His addiction meant that he was regularly fired from jobs: on at least one occasion he was reported to have attacked a colleague. Garavito was forced to move from job to job. He dreamt of returning home to kill his father, but never had the courage to do so.

He was now free, at least, to do as he pleased and meet whom he pleased. He associated with at least two women, one of whom he had met at a local church. The exact nature of their relationship is unclear – Garavito claimed not to have sexual relations with her, but he lived with her as if she were his partner, and she soon had a son. Certainly, the relationship never provided Garavito with any lasting happiness, and he soon drifted to the nearby city of Armenia, where he took a job in the bakery. He began to attend meetings at Alcoholics Anonymous, and was a regular at the local church. But he was unable to turn his life around; the twin urges to drink and have sex with young boys overpowered him. He would procure young male prostitutes in the local park, drink long into the night and then head to church in the morning, full of self-hate. He repented by quoting Saint Paul's letter to the Romans: 'For what I am doing, I do not understand; for I am not practising what I would like to do, but I am doing the very thing I hate' (Romans 7:15).

He found yet another job, this time in a local supermarket, and for a brief while his life improved. He met the second key woman in his life, Claudia, who already had two children, a boy of 14 and a young girl. By all accounts Garavito always treated the three of them well, but he could only ever be a husband and father figure to them, because his sexual interest remained with young boys. Many such children came into the supermarket, and Garavito's urge to molest them became an obsession. He described it later as a 'satanic force'.

Garavito the rapist

In October 1980, the terrible demons inside Garavito took full control, and he began his first wave of crimes. Over the course of the next 12 years he would rape some 200 children, lured from the chaotic streets of dozens of Colombian towns and villages. He favoured boys aged between eight and 13, ideally fair-skinned and blue-eyed. He lured them into the sugar-cane fields or to the quiet hillside coffee plantations, where he was hidden from view and could see anyone who might be approaching. His cover story was generally that he needed help with some task or other, and was prepared to pay the child 500 or 1,000 pesos if they would do a small job. Often he took the children by taxi from the town centre to the lonely outskirts,

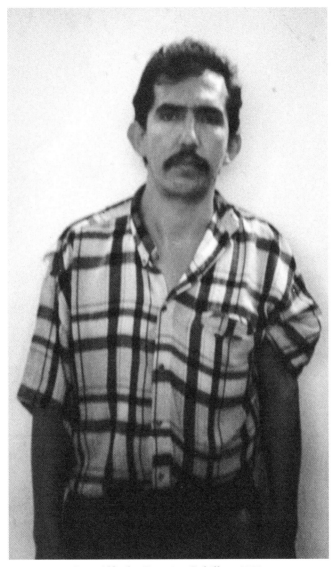

Luis Alfredo Garavito Cubillos, 1999

making friendly conversation during the ride.

He always approached his victims during daylight: for one thing, he was scared of the dark, and for another he knew that most children would not be missed for several hours during the day. It was entirely usual for children to help the family finances by selling lottery tickets and papers to adults, and Garavito's promise of money offered them a chance to knock off from their chores early and perhaps have an hour or two to themselves to play.

Garavito recognized that he needed help, and visited a psychiatrist. He could not bring himself to disclose the shameful details of his sexual impotence with women and attraction to young boys, however, and ended up being diagnosed with depression. In 1984, he was admitted to a psychiatric unit for 33 days, before being discharged to be treated thereafter as an outpatient. It didn't help. He avidly read books on black magic and the life of Adolf Hitler, and watched the film *The Silence of the Lambs*, which features a cannibalistic serial killer, five times. In 1986, he became obsessed with TV news stories of Campo Elías Delgado Morales, a teacher who murdered 28 people in the upmarket *Pozetto* restaurant in Bogotá before being shot by police. Garavito drifted to the city of Pereira and again formed a relationship with an older woman who had a son, Graciela Zabaleta. Again they lived together as if man and wife, though no sexual relations occurred.

His predatory sex crimes against children continued, and Garavito began to find that inflicting pain upon his victims was more gratifying to him than sex. He would bite the child's nipples and burn their buttocks before raping them. Over the course of the next eight years he raped on average one child a month, travelling throughout the coffee-growing regions of Circasia, Armenia, Calarcá, Pereira, Santa Rosa de Cabal and Manizales. He was briefly imprisoned for theft, but escaped detection for his more serious crimes until 4 October 1992.

By the time he was finally caught in the act of assaulting a child, Garavito was already guilty of a catalogue of heinous attacks that would mark him as the gravest kind of serial sex offender. Although consumed with self-hatred for committing the crimes, Garavito nonetheless meticulously recorded them all in a small, black book for his own twisted pleasure. He hadn't yet crossed the rubicon into murder, however, and a lengthy prison sentence at this point might have saved hundreds of young lives, but it was not to be.

The police officer who caught Garavito accepted a bribe in return for releasing him. Just two days later Garavito found a terrible new excitement, and the catalogue of murder began.

1992: A deal with the devil

In an interview after he was finally caught, Garavito would claim that his murder campaign began after he used a Ouija board to summon the devil. He felt a force possess him and a voice said 'What do you want? Do you want to serve me?' When he replied in the affirmative, a voice told him to go and commit his first murder. The location of this diabolic meeting was the largest city in western Colombia, Santiago de Cali, abbreviated by most Colombians to 'Cali'.

As places to make a deal with the devil go, Cali was an inspired choice: in 1992 it was as close to hell as anywhere on earth. The city was the stronghold of the notorious Cali drug cartel, described by the United States Drug Enforcement Agency as 'the most powerful crime syndicate in history'. The three leaders of the cartel were famous enough to be featured on the cover of *Time* magazine in July 1991. An uneasy alliance between the Cali cartel and Pablo Escobar's rival Medellin cartel to share the lucrative US cocaine market had collapsed, resulting in a deadly feud between the gangs.

In the 1980s the cartels had worked together to supply the CIA with the drugs that funded the 'Iran Contra affair', aimed at overthrowing the left-wing Sandinista government in Nicaragua. They had become too powerful for the local police to control. Each adopted a policy of *plata o plomo* ('silver or lead') towards the Colombian government – the silver being bribes for co-operation and the lead being bullets for resistance. The Medellin cartel blew up a Boeing 747 en route from Bogotá to Cali in the hope of killing a presidential candidate in 1989, killing 110 innocent people instead. Escobar's target was not on board, but two American civilians were, bringing Colombia's drug barons to the attention of US authorities. Escobar was now a wanted man in the eyes of the US, the Colombian government and the Cali cartel, and somewhat predictably he died from *plomo* to the head on 2 December 1993. This left the Cali cartel in control of 90 per cent of the world's cocaine market.

The marble citadels of the cartel's leaders loomed high above the sugar-cane fields of Cali. In such fields, and across the country, Luis Garavito would follow the satanic orders he believed he was given in Cali. He later testified that he couldn't remember the name of the first boy he killed, in the town of Jamundí just south of Cali, on 6 October 1992. He was Juan Carlos, a young local boy who just happened to pass by the bar in which Garavito was drinking. Garavito followed him, then approached him with the same story he had used countless times before. At a local store he stopped to buy 2 metres (6 feet 7 inches) of nylon rope, a bottle of cheap brandy and a butcher's knife.

Juan Carlos's body was discovered three days later. He had been raped and his penis had been cut off. Garavito later claimed the demonic voice had told him 'If you kill, many things will come to you'. He stated that he felt remorse and considered himself 'very evil' when he woke the next morning and realized his clothes were soaked in blood. But just six days later he would kill again, in the nearby city of Tulúa. The victim was 12-year-old John Alexander Penaranda and, like Juan Carlos, he was tied up, raped and stabbed to death. Garavito severed the fingers, thumbs and toes of his victims to make them look as though they were the subjects of satanic cults or the notorious *grupos de limpieza social* ('social cleansing groups'), both of which operated extensively in the area. The Cauca River, which flows through Cali, was known as 'The River of Death' due to the frequency with which bodies of *desechables* ('discardables') turned up in it. All too often these 'discardables' were street children. Garavito used this fact to his advantage, and it helps explain why he managed to avoid detection for so long.

He also moved around a great deal, and changed his appearance – often he would dress as a priest, and he had a range of different wigs, hats and glasses. Much of the time he would blend in on the streets by selling low-value products or religious items, his favourites being pictures of

Pope John Paul II and *El Nino Dios* (the baby Jesus). He would claim to be working on behalf of a religious foundation, and often used a false name.

1993: Becoming 'The Beast'

Garavito's murders became ever more frequent, and ever more gruesome. In 1993, he began a horrific new practice that would become a signature for almost all future killings: he disembowelled his victims whilst they were still alive. He frequently ended their torment by beheading them, and taking out their vital organs, which were almost never found. He butchered a total of 11 children in this fashion in 1993, moving between the capital Bogotá and the towns of Armenia, Quimbaya and Calarcá in the west. His last crime of that year was very nearly his last crime ever: in Tulúa, a 12-year-old victim fought back with a knife, severing the tendons in Garavito's thumb, before the child was overpowered and killed. His death was mercifully swift compared to the murderer's other victims.

The following year resulted in the murders of a further 27 children. He painstakingly recorded each and every killing in his notebook, and kept his bus tickets and newspaper clippings relating to the children in a black cloth bag. He would photograph many of the children before he attacked them and kept the photographs, too. Whenever the bag of mementos grew too unwieldy to carry, he would take it to his sister's house and leave it there. In 1995, whilst in Bogotá, Garavito fell and badly broke his leg. He walked with a distinctive limp from then on – a detail that helped lead to his eventual arrest. Garavito's murder rate also slowed, at least whilst he was still on crutches.

The following year, in Tunja, Garavito was arrested in connection with the disappearance of a local child, Ronald Delgado Quintero. His description matched that of an eyewitness. The smooth-talking serial murderer managed to convince the police that he was a poor, innocent street vendor who had been singled out because he was disabled. He was released. It was for the murder of this child that Garavito would eventually be convicted but that, alas, was many years in the future.

The killer changed his appearance once more, and stepped on to a bus heading north, to Risaralda. Ten year-old Jorge Andrés Brown Ramirez, who sold sweets to the passengers on such buses, would be his next victim. By the end of 1996, Garavito's notebook of death reached the grim milestone of 100 victims.

His name was now in the Colombian police system, at least – in so far as Colombia's police had a system in 1996. Nobody in the country had yet linked the disappearances of children in different provinces, and so there was still no co-ordinated investigation into the case. In fairness, what seems obvious in retrospect was not so clear at the time. Due to social problems in Colombia, children disappeared in far higher numbers than in more stable, developed countries. Parents often did not even report their offspring as missing, for fear of reprisals from cartels, criminals or corrupt police officials. When bodies were found well preserved, the fact they had been cut open led to suspicion that they were victims of the dark trade in human organs. But Garavito usually dumped the bodies of his victims in sugar-cane fields on the outskirts of the city, where the moist environment and activities of animals meant that often only scattered bones remained by the time they were found. This made identification of the victims all the more difficult.

It was only when playing children discovered a human skull in November 1997 that the hunt for the serial killer began in earnest. Police who arrived at the scene near Pereira soon discovered a mass grave containing the bodies of 36 children. Even in a country used to gruesome and violent crimes, it was a shocking discovery, and one that made headlines across Colombia.

By January 1998, the local police department had formed a task force, and it began to ask about any similar cases in other Colombian districts. Reports of mysterious mass disappearances of children poured in from the police departments of Meta, Cundinamarca, Antioquia, Quindío, Caldas, Valle del Cauca, Huila, Cauca, Caquetá and Nariño. There was no doubt, by now, that something was very wrong. However, the police still could not quite believe that a single man was responsible for so many deaths. They were soon contacted by a coroner in Palmira who disagreed. There, whilst committing one of his murders, Garavito had got sloppy.

The manhunt begins
In February 1998, in Buga, Garavito had lured a child to a paddock outside the city. As was his habit by now, having raped and murdered the boy, he lay beside the body for several hours drinking cheap brandy. On this occasion, however, he became so intoxicated that he passed out. A lit cigarette that he was smoking started a fire in the field. Garavito awoke to find himself ablaze, and surrounded by flames. In panic, he fled the scene – leaving behind a host

of vital clues. Police later recovered a pair of glasses, shorts, a comb, a screwdriver and a pair of shoes that were worn down in an unusual pattern.

Carlos Hernán Herrera, the Palmira coroner who examined the body recovered from the scene, concluded that a serial killer was responsible. He had seen similar patterns of violent dismemberment at other scenes in the vicinity: disembowelment, severed penises, and beheadings. By analysing the clues left behind, the coroner concluded they were looking for a man in his 40s who limped with his right leg. He wrote a report to the CTI (*Cuerpo Técnico de Investigación*, or technical investigation team), suggesting that a national manhunt needed to be launched urgently. The report sat in a drawer for another seven months.

More mass graves were uncovered in Colombia as the sugar-cane fields were cut and harvested. No doubt realizing that his crimes were beginning to attract attention, Garavito fled to the neighbouring country of Ecuador, where he continued his killing spree. With the aid of forged documents he assumed the identity of 'Bonifacio Morera'. He couldn't hide his thick Colombian accent, however, and when local children began to disappear, the limping foreigner drew the attention of the Ecuadorian police. Before they could mount an operation to capture him, however, he fled back to Colombia. Still the killings continued.

It was an extraordinary coincidence that eventually connected the name of Luis Garavito to the wave of murders. Detectives from the investigating team in Armenia were discussing the case when they happened to be over-heard by a secretary. She had previously worked in the city of Tunja, where Garavito had been arrested and questioned in 1996 over the disappearance of a child. He had fled that area after his release, but when the body of the child was found police had issued an arrest warrant for him. The secretary at Armenia had written that warrant in Tunja, and recognized the similarity between the Tunja and Armenia cases. The police began to investigate Garavito. They visited his sister, who informed them she didn't know his whereabouts but revealed that he had asked her to keep hold of some of his personal items. One of those items was the black cotton bag Garavito had stuffed full of mementos of his crimes. The bus tickets placed him at the time and place of each major crime scene. The police, finally, knew the identity of the killer.

The only problem being that they had no idea where Luis Alfredo Garavito Cubillos was.

Capture – and arrest

It was a taxi driver who first spotted a man emerging from trees in Villavicencio in April 1999. The authorities were on the lookout after two young boys had fled an attacker and alerted police. After searching the forest, the police had withdrawn to a safe distance in the hope of luring the culprit out. In the back of the police car sat twelve-year-old John Ivan Sabogal and his teenaged rescuer who, fortuitously, had been smoking pot nearby and helped facilitate the Sabogal's escape. They waited, ready to point out the perpetrator should he show himself. When Sabogal shouted 'That's him!', the police moved in. The man they detained claimed his name was Bonifacio Morera, and that he was lost after having got off the bus at the wrong stop.

Under intensive interrogation back at the police station,

the man stuck to his story. The police, armed with the unwavering testimony of the boy that the man had abducted, charged him with kidnap and attempted rape. The world's worst serial killer was behind bars, but at this stage only Garavito knew that the police had no idea that the prisoner they had been told was Bonifacio Morera was in fact responsible for hundreds of more crimes. That would become clear only three months later, at the CTI National Summit held in Pereira. There, detectives from across Colombia compared notes, photographs and fingerprints. The prints of Bonifacio Morera matched those of Luis Garavito, and the photographs confirmed that he was one and the same man.

On Friday 28 October 1999, 'Bonifacio Morera' was taken to court for what he believed would be a single charge of kidnapping and attempted rape. It was only when the judge bellowed 'Citizen Luis Garavito Cubillos, stand up!' that he realized his predicament. He was charged with a total of 118 murders. Shortly afterwards he would confess to all of them – and to 24 others that the police had not yet linked to him. He explained his system of recording each and every death in his notebook, with a horizontal line representing a victim. There were 140 such lines in the book. It is feared that there are other such 'little black books' that have never been found, and that Garavito may have killed as many as 400 children. In the end, on 13 December 1999, he was found guilty of 138 murders, and sentenced to a total of 1,853 years and nine days in prison.

But could be released any day now. The Colombian constitution, written amidst the bloody violence of 1991, was designed to protect its citizens from the worst excesses of corrupt and dysfunctional governments. As a result, it is one of the most liberal constitutions in the world. Not only is the death penalty prohibited, but life prison terms are, too. Sentences must be concurrent not consecutive, and the maximum sentence in 1999 was 30 years (since doubled to 60). Because Garavito pleaded guilty, the Superior Court of Bogotá reduced his sentence to 22 years in 2006. He is entitled to further reductions due to 'irreproachable conduct' during his time in prison. Working and studying in prison entitles inmates to a four-month reduction in sentence per year.

The same liberal constitution prevents the extradition of Colombian citizens to foreign countries – such as Ecuador, where Garavito faces a further 22-year prison sentence for the murders he committed there. If he walks free, he will follow in the footsteps of Pedro Lopez, the world's second-worst serial killer, also from Colombia. Lopez, 'the Monster of the Andes', was convicted of murdering 110 young girls in 1983, and walked free in 1998. He was required to report regularly to the authorities in order to continue his psychiatric treatment, but almost immediately disappeared. Interpol released an advisory notice for his re-arrest in relation to a fresh murder in his hometown of Espinal, Colombia, in 2002. His current whereabouts are unknown.

CHAPTER TWO

Eric Edgar Cooke, 'The Night Caller'

Australia Day, celebrated on 26 January each year, is the national holiday on which inhabitants of the 'Land Down Under' mark the anniversary of the arrival there of the First Fleet of British ships in 1788. It is generally a joyous event, and in 1963 it was especially sweet: Australia was in the middle of an economic boom, Prime Minister Robert Menzies had been in power since 1949 and no one in the country had ever heard of Eric Edgar Cooke. Today he is remembered as 'the Night Caller', and the murderous rampage on which he embarked that night is often cited as marking the end of an age of innocence.

In Perth, on the south-west coast of Australia, few people locked their doors at night in the 1960s. Crime rates were mercifully low and violent crime practically unheard of. Although almost 2 million live there today, it remains one of the most remote cities on earth, some 2,150 kilometres (1,335 miles) away from the next-nearest major city of Adelaide. Such isolation fosters a strong sense of community, and in 1963 the people of Perth believed that serial killers only operated far out to the east or south; their quiet, harmonious city was different, a haven of safety. Gunfire at around 2 am on 27 January 1963 shattered that illusion.

January is the height of summer in Australia, and in 1963, as usual in Perth, it was sweltering. The sea breeze is known as 'the Fremantle Doctor' for the relief it provides from the searing heat. Although it was now the early hours of the morning, many had stayed out to enjoy the holiday. One of them, a married businessman named Nicholas August, was the first to be shot. He was having an affair with 40-year-old Rowena Driscoll, then called Rowena Reeves, who was also hit by the same bullet. Nicholas had noticed a man watching as the lovers drank together in a parked car outside the Cottesloe Civic Centre. Speaking his mind, as most Australian blokes are wont to do, he suggested to the man that he might wish to 'piss off'. In response the man raised a .22 rifle and fired. The bullet passed through Nicholas's neck and into Rowena's wrist. Nicholas sped off as the mystery gunman fired at them again. Thanks to a different 'Fremantle doctor', this one at the local hospital, they both escaped with their lives.

Just around the corner on Broome Street, 29-year-old accountant Brian Weir was probably close enough to hear the shot. Moments later, Eric Cooke climbed on to a nearby garage roof opposite Weir's house, took aim and shot him in the head through a set of open doors. Weir was in a coma for six months and was left blind in one eye, deaf in one ear, paralysed and brain-damaged by the attack. He died three years later, after bullet fragments that had lodged in his brain caused a seizure. Cooke had not yet finished his murderous rampage: 18-year-old student John Sturkey was shot in the head later the same night as he dozed with his head towards the open verandah of his boarding house. His housemate was woken by his groans but thought he was having a bad dream, until she discovered him lying in a pool of blood.

Then retired grocer George Walmsley, 55, suffered a similar fate, gunned down as he answered the bell of his front door in the next street. His wife and daughter found him on the doorstep, unconscious, with a bullet hole in the centre of his forehead. Both of these last two victims died of their wounds. The banner headline of *The West Australian* newspaper on 28 January 1963 brought word of the carnage to the horrified people of Perth: GUNMAN STILL AT LARGE KILLS 2, INJURES 3.

As is often the case with serial murders, one avid reader who pored over every detail of the coverage was the man responsible for the random slayings, Eric Edgar Cooke. *The West Australian* was his favourite paper, and he had used the information in its pages to select victims in the past. Unbeknownst to Perth, Cooke was by this time no stranger to murder.

Early life

Eric Edgar Cooke was born on 25 February 1931 in the Victoria Park suburb of Perth, the eldest of three children. Like the vast majority of people who go on to become serial killers, he had an unhappy childhood. His father was a violent alcoholic, and young Eric bore the brunt of his rages. He was regularly beaten for no apparent reason, and found no break from his torment at school, where he was bullied due to his cleft palate and cleft lip ('hare lip'). Operations and speech therapy to fix these disorders were not yet available; consequently, for his entire life Cooke spoke in a low mumble. Academically gifted, he was nonetheless expelled from Subiaco primary school at the age of six for stealing from a teacher's purse. After bouncing around a series of different schools, and getting regularly caned for bad behaviour at all of them, he found work as a delivery boy at the age of 14. He joined the local Surf Lifesaving Club, but was asked to leave, ostensibly because he suffered blackouts but in reality because of a series of thefts from their lockers. One item Cooke stole was a watch, which he had engraved 'To Cookie from the boys of Scarborough Junior Lifesaving Club'.

By his mid-teens, Cooke had begun committing petty crimes to supplement his meagre wages, and this soon escalated to burglary, vandalism and arson. Breaking into homes was no longer enough: Cooke would slash the owners' clothes and bedding before setting fire to their house. The police caught up with him, and he was soon serving his first serious time in prison. He was paroled just three months in to his three-year sentence, because authorities were sympathetic to the young man's unfortunate family background. However, this conviction was to have disastrous consequences for Cooke: he had always dreamt of joining the Australian armed services, but his criminal record meant he was now not eligible to do so.

A changed man

On release from prison he appeared to be a changed man, rehabilitated by Methodist minister the Reverend George Jenkins. He began attending services at his local Methodist church, joined the hockey team and made new friends. The all-too-familiar compulsion to steal soon returned, however, and he was caught stealing from the church coffers. He also now saw the criminal opportunities presented by the wealthy western suburbs around the Nedlands Methodist Church, where many parishioners had welcomed him into their homes. He avidly read *The West Australian* newspaper, checking wedding notices to find where and when local brides would be away on honeymoon so he could break into their homes. Later, he would delight in reading reports of his murders and assaults in the same paper.

At the age of 21 he managed to sign up for the Australian Army by lying on his application form, and did well in training. He excelled especially in accurate shooting. However, his past criminal behaviour was discovered and Lance Corporal Cooke received a dishonourable discharge. Desperate not to lose the fellowship he enjoyed in the armed services, Cooke moved to Melbourne and joined the Reserve Army there. Again, he did well, and was popular with the other reservists. But once more his conviction was discovered and he was discharged. He returned to Perth, telling anyone who would listen that he had just returned from having fought heroically in the Korean War.

He became a truck driver to make ends meet, and in 1953 he was back at the Methodist church to marry a local waitress, Sarah Lavin, with whom he would have seven children. Despite this, he was arrested several times for voyeurism and prowling, and he also began to steal cars at night. It was easy to do because many residents left their cars unlocked with the keys in the ignition; Perth had not yet had its innocence taken from it. Back doors were left open and blinds were not drawn: it was the perfect environment for a thief and voyeur. Finally, in 1955, Cooke was sentenced to two years' hard labour after crashing a stolen car. By this time he was already on first-name terms with the local police, who believed him to be a petty criminal from an unfortunate background. They called him 'Cookie' and his glib sense of humour generally brought a grudging smile from those who arrested him.

The demon inside

But after his release from prison, Cooke's already tumultuous life began to spiral out of control. He would later sum up his motivation by saying: 'I just wanted to hurt someone'. In 1958, Cooke selected 26-year-old Dutch immigrant Nel Schneider to be the first person he hurt. By now an expert car thief, he stole a car and rammed it into the mother-of-two as she cycled down Hill View Terrace in the Bentley suburb of Perth. She was badly injured, and the attack left her with severe epilepsy for the rest of her life.

Two months later, in November 1958, Cooke broke into a house in the Applecross area, a favourite hunting ground of his. On this occasion he did more than steal: he fractured the skull of 15-year-old Mollie McLeod as she slept in her bed. It was symptomatic of a trend of increasing levels of sadistic violence from Cooke: one homeowner discovered Cooke had broken in and left their goldfish boiling in a pan on the stove. As Australian families gathered to celebrate Christmas, Cooke committed another hit-and-run attack. This time on Kathy Bellis, while she was returning home from a late shift at work in Belmont. She was left with a fractured skull and spine, broken pelvis, leg, kneecap and multiple lacerations. It was purely by good luck that she survived, but the evolution of Cooke's violence would reach its murderous climax just a few weeks into the new year.

First murders

Pnena Berkman, born Patricia Vinnicombe, woke to find Cooke burgling her apartment on the night of 30 January. The 33-year-old beautician tried to raise the alarm but Cooke caught hold of her and stabbed her to death with a stolen diving knife. The divorcée's eight-year-old son was not with her that night because it was the school holidays. Her neighbour, Joan Evans, thought she heard a scream but was told by her husband to go back to sleep. Cooke was left with numerous scratches to his face, which he would explain away as having been caused by his mentally disabled son Michael. And so Cooke got away with his first murder, leaving only a body and a mystery for the police to try and solve. They would soon have more of both: Cooke battered 17-year-old Alix Doncon in August, and then murdered for the second time in December.

His victim was wealthy 22-year-old Jillian Brewer, heiress to the fortune of Australia's 'Chocolate King' Sir Macpherson Robertson. The manner of her death was so horrific that a judge later refused to believe Cooke's confession. On 20 December 1959, Cooke watched as Jillian had sex with her boyfriend. Once the man had left, Cooke broke into the flat in Stirling Highway, Cottesloe, where his victim was sleeping. Her grey poodle, asleep under her bed, woke her by barking at the intruder. Cooke struck the woman just above her left eye with a hatchet he had stolen from a nearby garage. He then hit her twice in the throat. A further blow fractured her pubic bone and left a gaping wound between her legs. He then petted the dog to silence it, and went outside to dispose of the murder weapon. Having done so, he returned to the flat and poured himself a glass of lemonade from the fridge. He calmly drank it whilst listening to the 'rattling sound' of Jillian's every last gasp for air. Still conscious, she managed to ask 'Who is it?' as he walked back into her bedroom carrying a pair of dressmaking scissors he had found in the living room.

She was discovered by her boyfriend the next morning, lying on her back with her left arm lying across her chest. Cooke had stabbed her in the chest, abdomen, thighs and buttocks with the scissors. The police found them wiped clean and carefully placed back on a tray in the living room. There were no fingerprints – Cooke always wore women's leather gloves – and there was no sign of forced entry. Jillian, like many of her neighbours, had left her back door open. *The West Australian* headline on 21 December 1959 stated only 'GIRL (22) BEATEN TO DEATH IN HER FLAT'. The people of Perth did not yet know the full, shocking details of the sadistic killer who was prowling their streets. And even the police had not yet connected the hit and runs and assaults with the two murders.

On 9 April 1960, Cooke once again stole a car and mowed down a young woman with it. This time he knew his victim: it was 19-year-old Glenys Peak, to whom he had given lifts several times on prior occasions. He chatted to her about his mentally retarded son, and she later described him as 'a nice guy – you'd never take him for a murderer'. But Cooke's terrible compulsion by now had a hold on him, and the random attacks continued. He smashed his car into another woman, Jill Connell, a month later, seriously injuring her, and then ploughed into a trio of pedestrians shortly afterwards.

Because he was known to police as a habitual criminal, Cooke was questioned about the murder of Jillian Brewer after his arrest for burglary later the same year. However, investigators believed he was just a petty thief and not a violent murderer. Cooke spent another spell in prison for burglary, but there was nothing to connect him with any of the other crimes in Perth. Upon release he soon resumed his one-man campaign of terror.

In March 1962, Anne Whitsed awoke in her Nedlands apartment to find she could not breathe – something had been wound tightly around her neck and one of her arms was tied to the bed. Her cries alerted the neighbours and Cooke ran off. Peggy Fleury, a 25-year-old, was attacked in her North Cottesloe home in December of the same year. This time Cooke smashed his fist into her eye when she woke up as he sexually assaulted her. Again, her screams forced Cooke to flee as the young woman's parents rushed to her aid.

Then, on 26 January 1963, Cooke burgled a house in Como and stole a .22 calibre rifle and ammunition. The infamous Australia Day attack would finally bring him the attention he so desperately craved.

Australia Day aftermath

Perth changed overnight after Cooke's Australia Day attack. Stores sold out of guns and locks, and hundreds of dogs were bought – or adopted from the local pounds. Nobody left their homes unlocked or walked the streets at night. The pressure on the police to find the killer was immense, and in response they launched the largest manhunt in Perth's history and massively increased their visible patrols. Cooke had the good sense to lay low for a couple of weeks, and made a show of being concerned about the killer on the loose. He ordered his wife never to open the door unless she heard him whistle, and for several nights he insisted the entire family sleep in the same room for safety.

But secretly Cooke was revelling in his godlike power to instil fear, and could not resist striking again. On 9 February he ploughed a stolen car into 17-year-old Rosemary Anderson, one of the few women walking unescorted on the streets of Perth at this time. She had stormed off after an argument with her boyfriend, John Button, who found her lying by the road moments later. He put her in his car and drove to the hospital, but it was too late: Cooke had killed again. At the time police believed that it was Button who had mown her down, and he was convicted of her manslaughter. He served five years of a ten-year sentence and his conviction was finally quashed only in 2002.

John Button was a collateral victim of Cooke's actions: his next actual victim met her death just a week after Rosemary Anderson was killed. Social worker Lucy Madrill was found dead on her neighbour's lawn on 16 February. The 24-year-old's murder was not connected with Cooke's previous crimes because his method of killing had changed: this time he strangled his victim. He then dragged Lucy's dead body out of her bedroom and across the lawn at the back of her property, through a hedge to a neighbouring property. There he sexually assaulted her. A whisky bottle that he had inserted into her vagina was left in the crook of her left arm. The crime baffled the police, but did not appear to be related to the earlier shooting spree. On 10 August, however, the police and press alike were certain that the Australia Day shooter had struck once more: university student Shirley McLeod was shot in her home in the Dalkeith area of Perth. She had been babysitting at the property when Cooke took aim with his .22 rifle.

A lucky break

Six days later, the beleaguered police got an expected break. An elderly couple had been out walking on Rookwood Street in the suburb of Mount Lawley, a few miles east of the last crime scene. They stopped to admire the flowering Geraldton wax bushes that are native to western Australia, and suddenly noticed a rifle hidden amidst the foliage. They notified the police, who took the rifle away and performed a ballistics test on it. The results confirmed that it was the weapon used to kill Shirley McLeod. Since nobody had seen the person who hid the weapon, the police decided to set a trap and wait until the owner showed up to retrieve it. *The West Australian* newspaper agreed to run a story stating that the police were going to redouble their efforts in the Applecross and Mount Pleasant areas.

Cooke read the story and believed it was safe to return to his weapon cache in Mount Lawley, some way further to the east of the police presence. In the early hours of 1 September 1963 he slowly pulled up in a Holden sedan, checking the coast was clear. He did not spot the two detectives hiding behind camouflage netting. He was arrested by armed officers as he pulled the dummy rifle from the hedge. They searched him and found he was wearing women's gloves and had a pair of black women's panties in his pocket. He later admitted he had intended to use the gun to kill again that very night. It was Father's Day, and his children were waiting at his house to give him his present. He never came home again: it was a group of police officers who next arrived at the Cooke family's front door.

Cooke rapidly confessed to shooting McLeod, but insisted he had nothing to do with the Australia Day killings. Despite privately being sure they had their man, the police had little to tie the suspect to the earlier crimes. They decided to pander to his ego, taking him out for a chicken curry at the historic Albion Hotel in Cottesloe, close to where several of his most infamous crimes occurred. There, beneath the Tiffany chandeliers, Detective Max Baker laid it on the line to Cooke, telling him he was going to hang for killing McLeod so he may as well tell the truth about the other crimes, too. When he regained his composure Cooke nodded and agreed, saying 'I'm the bloke you're looking for'.

Then it was Cooke's turn to shock the police: he not only confessed to the shootings but informed them that he was also responsible for the hit-and-run incidents and assaults, too. One of the major problems the interrogators faced was that two of the crimes that Cooke confessed to had already been 'solved', as far as they were concerned. John Button was behind bars for killing his girlfriend, Rosemary Anderson, and a deaf-mute man by the name of Darryl Beamish had been convicted of the brutal murder of Jillian Brewer. The police decided that Cooke, a notorious liar, was trying to make himself look more important than

Eric Edgar Cooke, 1963

he really was, and refused to believe his confession. Tragically, Darryl Beamish would remain in prison for 15 years, and it would be a further 24 years before his conviction was finally overturned.

The Cooke legacy

In total Cooke confessed to eight murders and 14 attempted murders, plus more than 250 burglaries, each of which he managed to recollect with exceptional clarity. He was eventually charged with respect to the murder of student John Sturkey, the first to die in the Australia Day shootings, and at his trial he pleaded not guilty on the grounds of insanity. Cooke hoped to avoid the death penalty, but the jury rejected his claim to be of unsound mind and he was found guilty of wilful murder. On 27 November 1963 he was sentenced to death.

There was no appeal against the sentence, though Cooke had the right to one. On death row in Fremantle Prison, he was reunited with Reverend George Jenkins, the Methodist minister who had tried to rehabilitate him many years earlier. Cooke told him that he felt he deserved to hang, and expressed his concern that two innocent men were in prison for crimes he had committed. He swore on a Bible that he killed Jillian Brewer and Rosemary Anderson, and offered to testify to the fact under oath in court. But judges in the appeal courts decided the offer was just a tactic to postpone his execution.

Eric Edgar Cooke would be the 154th and final man to hang at Fremantle Prison. As was the custom, he was woken at 5.30 am on a Monday morning and transferred from cell number 12 to the condemned cell, ready to be

Eric Edgar Cooke spent his last days
on death row at Fremantle Prison.

hanged at 8 am. He was offered a glass of whiskey and allowed a few brief final words with his chaplain, George Jenkins. He had bidden his wife goodbye in the pale blue visiting room the day before, saying 'I'll never see you again Sal, because you'll be up there and I'll be down there'. As the prison clock struck 8 am on 26 October 1964, a hood was placed over the head of prisoner number 29050, and he went to his death with quiet resignation.

Cooke's wife Sally stayed with neighbours and the children had the day off school. A handwritten note on the Cooke family's front door asked the media to leave the family alone. They were already dealing with one bereavement – their eldest son, Michael, drowned while Eric was on death row. Despite this, a brick was thrown through their window and dozens of abusive letters sent to them. Fifty years later Sally Cooke told *The West Australian* paper, 'The best thing that ever happened to me was the day they hanged him'.

CHAPTER THREE

Peter Kürten, 'The Vampire of Düsseldorf'

'Aren't you afraid? So many terrible things have already happened here.'

Hubertine Meurer didn't answer. The man who had approached and spoken to her was a stranger, albeit a respectable-looking one. The question didn't require a response: in 1929 in Düsseldorf, after dark, everybody was afraid. A man known then as 'The Hammer Maniac' was terrorizing the city and had already killed six people that year – one of them at this very spot, just two weeks earlier. The 34-year-old quickened her stride along the isolated Hellweg, the main road through the Flingern district on Düsseldorf's eastern fringe, eyes fixed straight ahead. Seconds later, she was felled by a vicious hammer-blow to the skull. Three more such blows followed as she lay unconscious on the ground in a pool of blood.

Clara Wanders, a prostitute working on a street around the corner, was attacked just moments later. The killer used such force during his assault on her that the head of his hammer broke off; unlike the vast majority of his previous victims, the two women both survived the attacks.

Their testimonies were rushed off to the man leading the hunt for the maniac, Germany's most famous detective, Ernst Gennat.

Gennat was nicknamed 'Buddha', chiefly because of his vast 135 kilograms (297 pounds) weight, but because of his wisdom, too. He headed up Germany's newly established *Zentrale Mordinspektion* or central murder squad. The establishment of such a unit was one of many innovations that Gennat brought to German crime-fighting: he also pioneered the use of forensics and criminal profiling. Indeed, it was Gennat who first coined the term *Serienmörder* ('serial murderer') in 1930. The word was created to describe the man Gennat had pursued through the dark streets of Düsseldorf, Peter Kürten.

Childhood poverty – and violence
Peter Kürten was born in 1883 in Köln-Mülheim, Cologne, into a large and desperately poor family that all shared a single room. When his father was not in prison he would beat his wife and children during alcoholic rages, often threatening them with a knife. He forced his wife and 13-year-old daughter to have sex with him, often in front of the rest of the family. Peter learnt by example and had sexual relations with at least one of his sisters. His parents later divorced – a rare and extreme course of action in Germany at this time.

In the same building as the Kürtens lived a dog-catcher, who soon befriended Peter. The nine-year-old boy eagerly watched as the man explained how to masturbate and torture dogs. Before long, Kürten was experimenting with both sex and death himself in the local fields and stables.

He progressed from cutting the heads off dogs and geese to stabbing sheep as he had intercourse with them. At the age of 13 he had an orgasm whilst strangling a squirrel that was biting him, and from then on he became incapable of enjoying sex unless it involved pain and mistreatment.

He ran away from the family home soon afterwards, sleeping in vans and stealing in order to support himself. By the age of 15 he was serving his first prison sentence, for theft. By then, chillingly, he had already managed to get away with the first of his murders: at the age of just nine he drowned two boys whilst playing on a raft with them on the River Rhine. He was also a committed arsonist, confessing to four such crimes in 1904 – though in reality he had committed many more. He was in and out of prison several times between 1905 and 1913, mostly for petty crimes; in total he would spend more than 20 of his 47 years in prison. It was during one brief period of release that he committed his first documented murder as an adult.

It began as a straightforward robbery: Kürten broke into an apartment above an inn on Wolf Strasse, Cologne, in May 1913. He found ten-year-old Christine Klein asleep in her bedroom there. As Christine's parents served customers in the inn below, Kürten throttled the child in her bed, until her fingernails ceased scratching at his hands and her body went limp. Then he sexually assaulted her, dragged her head to the edge of the bed and cut her throat. He later described the delight it gave him to watch her blood spurt in great arcs over his hand and to listen to it drip onto a mat beside her bed. Though he dropped a handkerchief with the initials P.K. at the scene, the identity of Christine's killer would not become known for another 17 years.

In that same single year of freedom, he also attempted to strangle two women in remote locations, before breaking into another house and strangling a 16-year-old girl into unconsciousness. He wounded a man and a woman in two separate axe-attacks and attempted to butcher a sleeping child in a third. In addition, he launched numerous arson attacks, later expressing his disappointment that none of them resulted in anyone being burnt alive. Kürten evaded detection for all of these crimes.

But one thing even Peter Kürten could not escape was the outbreak of world war. In 1914 he was called up to fight for his country, but the slaughter of trench warfare was not the kind of violence that thrilled him. He soon deserted, and, as a result, was sentenced to seven years' hard labour: his first lengthy prison sentence. As 70 million combatants across the world fought one another to a bloody stalemate in the First World War, Kürten languished in solitary confinement in Brieg Prison (in modern-day Poland). There he achieved orgasms by dreaming of atrocities ('slitting up somebody's stomach, and how the public would be horrified'). He read voraciously of the crimes of Jack the Ripper in London, and fantasized about becoming such a notorious killer – or the chief detective who rids a city of such a scourge.

He was released in 1921, into a German society that had been ravaged by war and was desperate to heal its wounds and restore pride after a humiliating defeat. But Kürten was bent on wreaking revenge on a society he believed had brutalized him unjustly.

For a short period, Kürten appeared to settle down: he found permanent work in a factory and met and married a friend of his sister who had also served prison time (for shooting a former fiancé after he jilted her). Despite his marriage and new-found financial stability, however, Kürten continued to mistreat women violently in order to obtain sexual gratification, and he was briefly jailed in 1926. Upon his release nothing changed: he forced his wife to have sex when she didn't want it, and openly carried on affairs with other women, beating and choking them as he had intercourse with them. He threatened them with death if they went to the police. Eventually, two terrified servant girls reported Kürten's assaults on them and he was jailed again, for two months and then a further six months, in 1927 and 1928.

This catalogue of violent offences and murders, terrible though they were, served only as a prelude to the horrors that Peter Kürten would unleash in 1929. It was in that terrible year that he finally delivered on his promise to wreak revenge on society, and stain the dark streets of Düsseldorf red with blood.

1929 attacks

'Sometime around 6 o'clock I saw a woman going along the Bertastrasse. I went up to her and shouted "Stop!"' So begins Kürten's own account of his infamous murder spree. The woman he bumped into on 3 February 1929 was Maria Kuhn, though Kürten would only come to learn that by eagerly poring over the press reports of the attack later. Beyond wishing her good evening, he didn't speak to her before stabbing her 24 times with a pair of heavy Solingen Emperor scissors. 'I left her lying unconscious. I heard cries for help and made my way quickly down the

Hellweg,' he later said. Maria survived – just – but could give no detailed description of the man who attacked her on that dark winter evening. As she fought for her life in the hospital, her assailant revisited the scene of the crime several times, spontaneously achieving orgasms as he remembered what he had done there.

Five days later, Kürten would lead eight-year-old Rosa Ohliger by the hand down nearby Kettwiger Strasse, to a spot where the flickering gas lamps left large areas of the street in shadow. Her body was found under a fence by construction workers the following day. She had been stabbed 13 times and then set on fire. 'I wanted to increase the general indignation by setting light to the victim,' Kürten explained later, clearly concerned that the murder of a child would generate insufficient indignation on its own.

Only three nights passed in peace before 45-year-old mechanic Rudolf Scheer became the serial killer's next victim on 12 February. He had the misfortune to bump into Kürten whilst drunk, sometime around 8 o'clock in the evening. He was repeatedly stabbed in the neck and head, then rolled lifeless into a ditch. By next morning police had cordoned off the scene, just off the Hellweg – near where the first attack had happened. Again, Kürten returned to the spot to enjoy the outrage he had caused. A suspicious detective asked him how he had come to learn of the crime so soon, and he claimed that an acquaintance had telephoned him about it.

It would be over a year before the police got the chance to talk to the killer face to face once again.

In the meantime they arrested a 20-year-old local man with learning difficulties by the name of Johann Strausberg.

He rapidly admitted he was responsible for two incidents in which women were attacked with a noose. Under pressure, he falsely confessed to Kürten's crimes, too, and the police believed the case to be solved. But whilst Strausberg was confined in a mental asylum, three people were stabbed with a dagger in separate attacks on the night of 21 August. Anna Goldhausen was stabbed in the left breast as she walked along Erkrather Strasse just after 10 pm, then Olga Mantel was stabbed twice in the back on the same street shortly afterwards. At around 2.30 am, Kürten watched an ambulance take away his third victim of the night, Gustav Kornblum, whom he had stabbed in the back a little earlier.

It was not yet obvious to the police that Strausberg was not the killer they were hunting. The weapon used in the attacks on 21 August was a dagger, not the scissors used in the previous attacks. It seemed to them that an entirely separate maniac was now on the loose. Then, on 25 August, the bodies of five-year-old Gertrude Hamacher and her 14-year-old foster sister, Louise Lenzen, were found on allotments close to their home in the Flehe district of the city. Both had been strangled and stabbed before having their throats cut. On the same day as their bodies were found, 26-year-old Gertrud Schulte was taken to hospital with 13 stab wounds after being attacked near Neuss, just outside Düsseldorf. A man using the name 'Fritz Baumgart' had tried to have sex with her, and when she told him that she would rather die he replied, 'Well die then!' before plunging a knife into her.

On Monday 30 September, another body was found, this time in a meadow on the outskirts of Düsseldorf.

Domestic servant Ida Reuter had been beaten to death with a hammer. The change of weapon led the police to assume that this case was not related to the others, and that yet another killer was now on the loose. This new killer struck again on 12 October: unemployed servant girl Elisabeth Dorrier was found unconscious in the Flingern district at first light, and later died of hammer wounds to her left temple.

Journalists from around the world now descended on Düsseldorf to cover the unfolding hunt. The panicked public deluged the police with tip-offs, often by post, and hoaxers wrote letters claiming to be the killer. Gennat's team had to sift through 13,000 letters in the course of the enquiry. An additional problem was false confessions: no fewer than 200 people gave themselves up to the police, claiming to be the killer. The popular crime monthly *Kriminal Magazin* ('The Criminal Magazine') summed up the mood: 'Düsseldorf is at fever pitch! The Rhineland is trembling with excitement! ... Germany is tumbling these days from one sensation to another ... A mass murderer is playing with the city.'

Kürten, who had dreamt for so long of exactly this kind of attention, was happy to play along with the dark game that the press had identified. The day after he killed Elisabeth Dorrier, he sent a letter to the police, in which he marked out the location of a further body that they had yet to discover. They visited the spot they believed the letter referred to, but found nothing. It was two weeks later that Hubertine Meurer was attacked by a well-spoken man as she walked along the Hellweg in the same area – by the man who first asked her 'Aren't you afraid?'

On Saturday 9 November, the body of five-year-old Gertrud Albermann was found amidst rubble beside a factory yard on the outskirts of Düsseldorf. She had been strangled, stabbed and sexually assaulted. With one or more killers clearly still on the loose, and the entire city now engulfed in terror, the elite murder squad from Berlin was sent to Düsseldorf to help.

Gennat's murder squad

One of Kürten's recurring fantasies was that the people of Düsseldorf would stage a torchlit procession in his honour after he had rescued the city from a monstrous killer. The man tasked with saving the city for real, Ernst Gennat, arrived in Düsseldorf with no clear leads to follow. The local police were disorganized and poorly trained. Gennat brought to the inquiry more than just his Daimler-Benz Mordauto ('Murder car'), which converted into a mobile office to record clues in detail directly at a crime scene. More importantly he brought experience of hunting, and capturing, a serial killer like Kürten. Though at first the crimes were not connected by police, as the body count in 1929 rose it became apparent that one man was responsible for several of the incidents. Gennat had interviewed 'The Werewolf of Hannover', Fritz Haarmann, who had been captured four years earlier after murdering 24 men, often by biting through their throats. He had investigated 'The Berlin Butcher' Carl Großmann, who had murdered and cannibalized at least 26 people before hanging himself in a police cell whilst awaiting execution. Indeed, it was cases such as these that had persuaded Gennat of the need

Ernst Gennat (far left), director of the Berlin criminal police, led the investigation for the 'Vampire of Düsseldorf'

for a specialized homicide unit in Germany.

But the Düsseldorf case was different, unlike anything even the ace detective Gennat had seen before. Haarmann's victims had all been homosexuals; Großmann killed vagrants and prostitutes. The Düsseldorf killer had already murdered women, children and a man, and attacked many others, all apparently at random. There appeared to be no pattern, and as a result the then much-favoured method of using undercover police as bait for a killer was useless. Gennat was famous for his methodical approach to collecting evidence, but he was operating in a world before DNA testing: the semen collected from the underwear of Rosa Ohliger told him only that the motive for the crimes was sexual; it gave no clue about the identity of the offender.

The police had tried to keep the latest hammer attacks quiet from the press, concerned that the public would become hysterical if they learnt of even more victims. In private, also Gennat railed against the 'mass psychosis' that appeared to have gripped the city. But he began to use the press to entrap the killer, aware that the perpetrator of these crimes was probably following the investigation in the papers. At a series of press conferences, Gennat compared the Düsseldorf killer to Jack the Ripper, saying London's infamous murderer 'was a mere beginner compared with his Düsseldorf disciple'. Doubtless Kürten, who had long idolized Jack, was delighted. But Gennat was determined that, unlike the Ripper, the Düsseldorf killer would not evade justice. A reward of 15,000 German marks (around £40,000 or $62,000) was offered for information that led to the capture of the killer – a vast sum in Germany during the Great Depression. Gennat stated his belief that the suspect would be undone by his love of publicity. It may have been a deliberate ploy on the detective's part to try and goad the killer into contacting him directly: by this time Kürten, frustrated at the lack of coverage of his latest crimes, had begun communicating with the press.

In early November, Kürten wrote to the one of the newspapers that had been most vocal in its criticisms of the investigation thus far. He enclosed another map showing the location of the same undiscovered body he had referenced previously. Across the map was written 'Murder at Pappendelle. In the place marked with a stone lies a buried corpse'. The police, now under Gennat's control, scoured the entire area and located a straw hat and set of keys, found by a farmer in his field in Pappendelle. Photographs were published in the papers and a woman came forward claiming they belonged to her housekeeper, Maria Hahn, who had been missing since 11 August. Soon after, the police found the location referenced in the mysterious map. As the author had claimed, a body was buried there. It was Maria Hahn. She had suffered multiple stab wounds to her forehead and body.

For the rest of the year, the police searched for the missing handbags of victims Dorrier and Reuter, and for Schulte's purse. A mannequin dressed in Dorrier's clothes was toured around Düsseldorf's cabarets and dance halls. Graphologist Dr Hans Schneikert examined the hundreds of letters received and decided that two were written by the person who had written the November map letter. But the trail went cold, and the attacks stopped as winter closed in.

They would begin again, however, in spring 1930. In Grafenberg woods on the eastern fringes of the city, three women survived rape and strangulation attempts. Hildegard Eid on 23 February and Marianne dal Santo and Irma Becker in March. In April, five similar attacks were reported by women; all of the victims survived to tell their tales.

Then, on 30 April, in the same woods, Charlotte Ulrich was attacked with a hammer and left for dead. On waking in a pool of her own blood, she staggered to a nearby railway station to get help. She was wanted by the police for theft so did not contact them, instead she recuperated without medical attention at the home of two benevolent strangers. Incredibly, despite having a severely fractured skull, she made a full recovery. When she did finally come forward to give details of the horrific attack, she was jailed for three months. By then Kürten had struck again.

The Büdlick attack

Maria Büdlick was waiting at Düsseldorf train station, and getting increasingly concerned. A woman she had met on the train, Frau Brucker, was supposed to meet her in order to help her find accommodation. She hadn't turned up and it was getting late. Düsseldorf was the last place on earth where any woman would want to be alone and without a place to stay. She was approached by a well-dressed and polite man who offered to show her to the local women's hostel. As he led her through the city's Volksgarten park, however, she became afraid, and refused to go any further. The man became angry with her and told her she was being ridiculous. Attracted by his raised

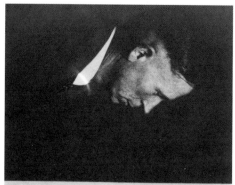

Mug shots of Peter Kürten, 1931

voice, a second man approached, and Maria Büdlick's would-be escort disappeared into the shadows. The second man informed her she was right to be worried – the women's hostel was in the opposite direction to the way she was being led. She gratefully accepted his offer to show her the right way. The man who took her into the park was never traced.

The man who escorted her back out of the park was Peter Kürten.

They talked en route, and Büdlick accepted Kürten's offer to return to his three-bedroom house in Mettmanner Strasse where he said his wife would prepare her something to eat. Büdlick was led instead to an empty one-bedroom attic flat, where Kürten gave her milk, bread and ham. From there, he escorted her on to a tram to take her to the hostel. The tram headed out of town and they got off near some woods, which Büdlick was told was a shortcut to the hostel. In the woods Kürten raped her whilst holding her throat. For some reason, which even he himself could not later explain, he did not then kill her. Instead, he asked her if she could remember where he lived, and when she said no, he let her go. It was not, as Detective Gennat had predicted, Kürten's thirst for publicity that led to his capture, but this single inexplicable act of mercy.

A traumatized Büdlick wrote a letter to the woman she was due to meet at the station, explaining what happened. But she misspelt the woman's name, and the letter ended up in the hands of a woman named Brugman rather than Brucker. Frau Brugman took the letter to the police, who tracked Büdlick down. On 21 May 1930, Büdlick took them back to the house of the man who had attacked her.

From his balcony at number 71 Mettmanner Strasse, Peter Kürten recognized Büdlick and immediately slipped out of the house, eluding the two detectives who were waiting outside.

But Kürten must have known that he was now on borrowed time. On Friday 23 May, detectives went to the workplace of Kürten's wife, who informed them that her husband had arranged to meet her at the Church of St Rochus at 3 pm the next day. And then she dropped a bombshell: the day before, he had confessed to her that he was the Düsseldorf mass murderer.

On Saturday 24 May, the police surrounded the church square and arrested Kürten without a struggle. He immediately confessed. He recalled in vivid detail each of his crimes, and even admitted to drinking the blood of his victims. Over the course of the following week he led police to a bush in a park where he claimed to have hidden the two hammers he used in the attacks. They were not there but a police appeal soon resulted in two local boys handing them in. Kürten also pointed out where he had hidden the handbags of Reuter and Dorrier. It was only then that Gennat was fully satisfied that he had, finally, caught the killer.

'Is this what a murderer looks like?'

That was the question asked by one court reporter when he and the general public finally got a look at the man who had confessed to the crimes. At that time it was generally believed that criminals were 'primitives', subhuman types whose physical features were reminiscent of apes. Kürten was dapper, handsome, immaculately dressed: he was 'normal'.

The trial opened on 13 April 1931, nearly a year after Kürten's arrest. The courtroom was the drill hall of Düsseldorf police headquarters, presided over by three judges. The dock had been hastily constructed for the occasion and resembled a wooden cage. A room next door was crammed with grim exhibits – several of the victims' shattered skulls, the various weapons Kürten used in the crimes and articles of clothing worn by the victims. He was charged with ten murders and seven attempted murders; 40 arson cases he had confessed to were omitted. He was found guilty of nine of the murders and sentenced to death by guillotine for each. Weimar Germany had not carried out an execution since 1928. As he awaited sentence, Kürten was bombarded with love letters and requests for autographs – as well as hate mail expressing the view that he deserved a long, lingering death and would shortly suffer for eternity in hell. He petitioned the Prussian justice minister for a reprieve in June, but the petition was declined. He was executed the day after he received the news, on Thursday 2 July 1931.

One of the questions Kürten asked the psychiatrist who interviewed him was whether he would be able to hear the sound of his own blood gush when the blade severed his head. He remarked that, for him, this would be the ultimate thrill.

Killers on display

The cannibal 'Werewolf of Hannover' Fritz Haarmann is featured, 'Where's Waldo?' style, on the local tourist board's annual advent calendar, and his story is told to tourists on the city's guided tours. Other killers seem to forgotten lost in the passage of time, or perhaps we forget them because we need to, so terrible are their crimes. Who now, outside of the former Prussian town of Münsterberg (now Ziebice, Poland), remembers Karl Denke, the man who killed at least 42 people and turned their skins into belts and braces? It was not Denke but Peter Kürten, 'The Vampire of Düsseldorf', who was destined to become the poster-boy of evil in the Weimar Republic of the 1920s. And that is exactly the way that Kürten would have wanted it; indeed he planned it that way from the start. Denke was a social outcast with a low IQ, a loner who preyed on vagrants and those marginalized by society. Kürten was 'one of us': intelligent, eloquent and immaculately turned out. He was immortalized first of all in director Fritz Lang's classic 1931 film M – at the time perceived as too shocking and controversial to be shown in Düsseldorf. Later, Detective Gennat and the psychiatrist Karl Berg both wrote about their involvement in the case, ensuring that Kürten would haunt the world from beyond the grave. It was only much later, however, that the moniker 'The Vampire of Düsseldorf' stuck.

Kürten haunts not just from the page but from behind a perspex screen: his severed, mummified head revolves on a hook in a display case in the *Ripley's Believe It Or Not Museum* in Wisconsin, United States. Doctors examined it after his death in order to try to find out if some kind of abnormality had caused his murderous fury. The brain was found to be normal.

CHAPTER FOUR

Tsutomu Miyazaki, 'The Otaku Murderer'

Many countries around the world look enviously towards Japan and ask the same question: how have they managed to create such an apparently harmonious and crime-free society? The crime rate in Japan is, by all modern standards, staggeringly low, and the rate of violent crime lower still. Fewer than one person is murdered for every 100,000 in the population, compared to 4.8 for the United States and 44.7 in Belize; only Iceland, with a population of 325,000, has a lower homicide rate than Japan, where 127 million live. Not only that, but the rate in Japan is actually falling, whilst in most other countries the already high homicide rate continues to climb. As a rule, then, Japan does not suffer from the curse of the serial killer. The exception to that rule was Tsutomu Miyazaki.

There are devils about

She was wearing a pink and white T-shirt with cats on it. Pink pumps. She had a pageboy haircut, and was 105 centimetres (3 feet 4 inches) tall. On 23 August 1988, in Saitama, just north of the capital Tokyo, everyone was looking for four-year-old Mari Konno. Her father had reported her missing the day before, after she failed to return from a trip to play at a friend's house.

From the outset, the Japanese police treated her disappearance as a murder case. Girls of that age simply do not disappear in Japan. Police squad cars prowled the streets, their loudspeakers warning parents to keep their children indoors. Every home in the area was visited by officers, and 50,000 posters of Mari were distributed. Two boys and a 38-year-old housewife had independently seen the missing girl with a man dressed in a white sweater and white slacks. He had a round, pudgy face and curly hair. That was all the police had to go on: despite an extensive search with dogs, no trace of Mari could be found.

Yukie Konno, Mari's mother, went on television to appeal for help, and expressed hope that her daughter might still be alive. A couple of days later she received an anonymous postcard bearing the message: 'There are devils about'. Although the police dismissed it as the work of a crank, the card was sent by the killer, Tsutomu Miyazaki.

The outsider
Tsutomu was born prematurely in Itsukaichi, Tokyo, on 21 August 1962. He weighed just 2.2 kilograms (4 pounds 8 ounces) and the joints in his hands were fused together, meaning he could not bend his wrists upwards. He was teased about his deformity from an early age and rapidly became acutely self-conscious. At school he was remembered by classmates and teachers alike as a loner who found it impossible to make friends. Later, at college, he took his video and still camera to the tennis courts to take 'upskirt'

photographs of the female players. One of his own sisters caught him spying on her in the bath.

Though bright, Tsutomu lost interest in his studies as he grew older and was forced to abandon his plan to enter Meiji University due to poor grades. Instead, he found work at a printing company that belonged to a friend of his father and read comic books voraciously when not at work.

His father, Katsumi Miyazaki, owned the *Akikawa Shimbun*, a local Itsukaichi newspaper, and was well-regarded in the locality. Like many Japanese men, he was something of a workaholic, and often absent from the family home that Tsutomu continued to share with his parents. The only person with whom Tsutomu bonded was his grandfather, Shokichi, and it was the old man's death in May 1988 that appears to have triggered Tsotumu's descent into madness and murder. In later letters, Tsutomu Miyazaki claimed to have eaten some of his grandfather's cremated remains in order to try and reincarnate him. By now 25 years old, and with no ability to form adult relationships, Tsutomu turned to child pornography and lolicon anime (a genre of Japanese comic depicting sexualised prepubescent girls) for his thrills. He began to amass a vast collection of videos and comic books, many either sexual or violent in nature. When the police searched his room after his eventual arrest they found 5,763 such videos, as well as hundreds of comic books.

On 21 August 1988, Tsutomu Miyazaki celebrated his 26th birthday. The next day, he drove away from the family home in his Nissan Langley sedan and stopped shortly afterwards to offer a ride to four-year-old Mari Konno.

The murders

Once the girl was inside his car, Miyazaki drove for more than an hour and a half to a quiet woodland area 50 kilometres (31 miles) from Saitama. He claimed the two of them chatted happily during the journey but only he knows whether that is true. What is beyond dispute is that the pair walked through the woods, away from the hiking paths that crisscross the area, to a remote part of the forest where they could not be seen or heard. There, Miyazaki strangled the girl to death before undressing and sexually assaulting her. Before and after the crime he took photographs in order to document his atrocity. He left her body in the woods, bundled up her clothes and returned to his car. Nobody had seen him enter the woods and nobody saw him leave. Nor did anyone see him re-enter the woods six weeks later, with seven-year-old Masami Yoshizawa.

Masami was lured into Miyazaki's car from a quiet street in Hanno, close to where he lived. She met the same terrible fate as Mari, who still lay less than 100 metres (just over 100 yards) away; strangled, stripped and sexually assaulted. Again, Miyazaki obsessively photographed his own crime scene. As he took pictures of Masami's body, a muscle spasm caused her corpse to twitch, and he fled the scene in terror.

The police repeated the same diligent process they had undertaken after Mari's disappearance, conducting house-to-house enquiries and papering the city with posters of the missing Masami. They suspected a connection between the disappearances of the two children, but had no leads to follow, no suspects to pursue. One of the disadvantages of an incredibly low crime rate is that no officers gain experience in hunting down serial killers – but even seasoned specialists would have struggled with so little to go on, as in this case. At this point, neither body had been found – and both cases were officially missing persons enquiries. Two months later, that would change.

Erika Namba was returning from a friend's house in Kawagoe, Saitama, when Miyazaki pulled over and offered her a lift. The four-year-old was reported missing by her anxious parents later the same day, 12 December. Both they and the police must have feared the worst, given the previous disappearances in the area. The next day, a worker at a local Youth Nature Facility found clothing belonging to a child in woods behind a parking area. The police raced the 50 or so kilometres (30 miles) to the scene and conducted a thorough search of the entire area. Erika's body was discovered the next day in a different part of the woods. She had been bound by the hands and feet with nylon cord, strangled and sexually assaulted.

Once these details were made public, two men came forward to state that they had been in the area at around the time that Erika went missing. They remembered helping a man whose Toyota Corolla car had got stuck just off the road, very close to where the corpse was found. The car was parked with its hazard lights flashing, so they stopped to take a look. A man came out of the woods, carrying a crumpled sheet. As he placed the sheet in the boot of his car, he explained he had accidentally driven off the road and become stuck in guttering. The men were too polite to ask what he had been doing in the woods with a sheet: they had simply helped him lift the car out and he drove away. What struck them as most odd about

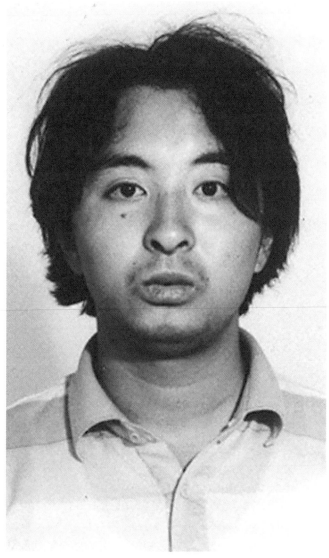

Tsutomu Miyazaki

the incident at the time was the fact that the man did not offer them a word of thanks. When pressed, they recalled that the car had plates identifying it as originating from Hachioji, Tokyo.

Toyota Corollas are one of the most popular cars in Japan. The police checked some 6,000 that might have been the one the men spotted, but they drew a blank. It turned out that the witnesses were mistaken: it was not a Toyota Corolla they had lifted out of the gutter on that fateful December night, but a Nissan Langley. The ungrateful man they had helped was Tsutomu Miyazaki. He had had an amazingly lucky escape; the police had come agonizingly close to catching a mass murderer. Instead, Miyazaki continued to live his lonely life of comic books and murder, while families across Japan kept their children indoors and drove them to and from the school gates each day.

The killer makes contact

The families of the murdered children soon began to receive mysterious silent phone calls. When they answered, they could hear someone on the line but nobody spoke. If they ignored the phone it would ring insistently, for as long as 20 minutes. And then, even more chillingly, mysterious postcards began to arrive. Erika Namba's father, Shin'ichi, received one a week after her death that said: 'Erika. Cold. Cough. Throat. Rest. Death'. It was a sick, taunting and sadistic move on the part of Miyazaki. But the parents of still-missing Mari Konno were to receive an even more macabre communication from the killer. Mari's father, Shigeo, found a cardboard box on his doorstep as he left for work at around 6 am on 6 February 1989.

Tsutomu Miyazaki had returned several times to the spot where the bodies of Mari and Masami lay decomposing in the dark woods 50 kilometres (31 miles) from their anguished loved ones in Saitama. On one visit, he cut off Mari's hands and feet, and kept them as souvenirs. The rest of her body he burnt. The ashes that remained he placed into a box, along with ten of her baby teeth and photographs of her clothing. On top of these he placed a single sheet of copier paper bearing the words 'Mari. Bones. Cremated. Investigate. Prove'. This was the box that Mari's father found on his doorstep. He immediately turned it over to the police.

Dr Kazuo Suzuki of the Tokyo Dental University examined the teeth and, at a police press conference, announced they did not belong to Mari Konno. Mari's mother, at the same press conference, spoke of her faint hopes that her daughter was still alive. In his room, alone as usual, Miyazaki watched in disbelief. He wrote a three-page letter to the Konno family, and the local press, entitled 'Crime Confession'. He reiterated that he had killed all three of the girls, and that the remains in the box belonged to Mari. He claimed he did not want her mother to continue to have false hope. The letter was signed 'Yuko Imada', a girl's name but also a pun in the Japanese language, meaning 'Now I have courage' and also 'Now I will tell'.

Shortly afterwards, Dr Suzuki reversed his opinion on the teeth, and police forensic experts confirmed that they did, indeed, belong to Mari. Her case was officially changed to a homicide investigation, and linked to the murder of Erika Namba. What the press and public had speculated on for so long was finally confirmed: a serial killer was at work in Saitama.

Clues

Although handwriting experts were unable to provide police with much useful information after analyzing the letters, the communications nonetheless gave investigators some vital leads. They were able to establish that the photographs had been taken with a relatively rare Mamiya 6 x 7 format camera, the kind used by professional photographers or printers rather than hobbyists. The cardboard box was double-walled and corrugated: it was the kind used to ship fragile objects such as camera lenses. The typeface on the postcards came from a phototypesetter, and an industrial copier would also have been required to produce them. This set of clues ought to have been enough for the police to focus in on those working in professional print shops in the area. Had they done so, they would soon have come face to face with the quiet loner Tsutomu Miyazaki. For reasons that remain unclear, this never happened. The police distributed copies of the 'Crime Confession' letter to local houses in the hope of someone coming forward with new information. The Konno family buried their daughter and appealed to the killer to return her hands and feet, so that she could walk and eat in heaven.

What they got in response, however, was not more of their daughter's remains but more of the killer's twisted letters. Miyazaki, again signing himself as 'Yuko Imada', wrote saying that he had wanted to fold her arms across her chest but rigor mortis had set in. He then documented how red spots had appeared on her body as she decomposed;

how those red spots had reminded him of the *Hinomaru* or 'Circle of the Sun' on the Japanese national flag; how the body had liquefied and begun to smell. Clearly, the killer enjoyed reliving his experiences both in person and on paper, and the outrage and pain he would cause the parents of his victim seemed to extend the duration of his pleasure. In the end, however, he still desired fresh victims. By 1 June 1989, Miyazaki was skipping work to try to capture more children. He persuaded a small child playing near a school to take off her underwear while he photographed her. Spotted by neighbours, he was chased off before he could do anything even worse. But he managed to escape from the scene before the police arrived. It was, for him, another lucky escape. For five-year-old Ayako Nomoto, it meant she had five days left to live.

The cannibal killer

The little girl was playing alone in a park in Ariake, near Tokyo Bay. Miyazaki approached her and asked if he could take her photograph. Within a few moments she was in the back of his parked Nissan Langley. According to Miyazaki's later testimony, she fought hard as he strangled her, kicking her legs furiously. But the struggle was unequal, and after four or five minutes the kicking stopped and she became limp. He bound her hands and feet, placed tape over her mouth, wrapped her in a sheet and placed her in the boot of his car. Miyazaki had macabre plans for her even after her death.

He rented a video camera and returned home. There, he stripped Ayako's body and recorded himself sexually abusing her. He hacked off her head, hands and feet, and dumped her torso beside a public toilet in the Miyazawa-ko cemetery in Hanno. In his back garden, he then roasted the little girl's hands and ate some of the flesh from them. He hid the rest of her remains in a wooded hill beside his house, before thinking better of it and retrieving them to keep in the storeroom behind his bedroom. He later scattered them more widely in the woods and burnt the sheets he had used to wrap the body. Ayako's torso was quickly discovered, and she was identified by matching her stomach contents with her family's report of her last meal.

Tsutomu Miyazaki's crimes were becoming more demoniacally elaborate, and showed no sign of slowing down. He was, in every sense, remorseless. Just a few days later, on Sunday 23 July 1989, he prowled the streets again, this time fixing upon two young sisters playing together in Hachioji, about 40 kilometres (25 miles) west of central Tokyo.

The eldest of the children informed her father who ran in wild panic through the streets of Hachioji to the spot where his daughter said a young man had approached them. He found his younger daughter in the back of Tsutomu Miyazaki's car, naked and terrified as Miyazaki photographed her genitals. The father landed a blow to Miyazaki's head that knocked him to the ground, but he managed to stagger away from the scene as the father tended to his screaming daughter. The police were on the scene in minutes, but the assailant had escaped down a swampy riverbank. As officers swarmed over the car, and radios crackled with descriptions of the wanted man, Tsutomu Miyazaki brazenly returned to collect his vehicle. He was immediately arrested. One of the largest manhunts in modern Japanese history ended with the suspect simply walking up to the police in the centre of a major city.

The police were caught so off-guard that the press beat them into Miyazaki's room, filming inside it before it had been cordoned off for the forensic team to do their work. The coverage focused on the man's apparent obsession with comic books and videos, leading him to be dubbed 'The Otaku Murderer'. The closest English translation of '*otaku*' would be 'nerd' or 'geek': one who has unhealthy, obsessive interests, especially in the Japanese anime and manga comic books. The murders fuelled a moral panic against the anime and manga culture or 'fandom' in Japan, though there was never any proof of a direct link between Miyazaki's horrific crimes and the content he watched and read.

When the police did gain access to the bedroom, however, they found videos of Mari Konno amidst the vast collection of tapes. In the days that followed, the suspect made a full confession, and showed the police where the bodies of the missing girls lay. His parents went into hiding and his father refused to pay for a defence lawyer, insisting it would be unfair on the victims, so a state lawyer was appointed. The trial began on 30 March 1990.

Trial and execution

More than 1,500 people queued outside the Tokyo district court building to see first-hand what the notorious 'Otaku Murderer' really looked like. Just 50 or so were let in, and even these 'lucky' few would be disappointed to see the young, round-faced defendant scribbling cartoons and falling asleep during the hearings. When the 'killer geek' did speak, it was to demand the return of his car and his beloved collection of videos and books.

In Japan, until 2009, there were no jury trials: a panel of judges decided Miyazaki's fate. Loyalty to fellow colleagues is one of the defining characteristics of Japanese society and judges and prosecutors are essentially colleagues working for the Ministry of Justice. From 1991 to 2000, more than 99 per cent of defendants in Japan were convicted. Thus, a defendant's attorney would be faced with an uphill battle to obtain a not-guilty verdict.

Much of Miyazaki's trial was shaped, not by the determination of innocence or guilt, but by the debate over whether he was sane or insane: if he was deemed to be mad he would escape the death penalty. Psychological assessments were ordered. Miyazaki claimed that a demonic creature called 'Rat Man' had taken possession of his mind, and three court-appointed psychiatrists found him to be mentally unsound, though they disagreed over whether he was schizophrenic or suffering from multiple personality disorder. In the end, the judges came to the conclusion that he was not so mad that he could not hang, and he was sentenced to death. In response to being found guilty, Miyazaki penned a letter to his father, Katsumi Miyazaki, angrily blaming him for all of his crimes. Katsumi expressed his regret at not taking more notice of his son's early antisocial behaviour and inability to make friends. Having made his public apology, he then killed himself by jumping into a river in 1994. His son remarked that he 'felt refreshed' upon hearing the news.

Japan is one of the few industrialized countries that maintains the death penalty (along with the United States and South Korea, though the latter currently has a moratorium in effect). Human rights organizations have long criticized Japan for its lack of transparency over executions, which are carried out in secret and at short notice. Those on death row are not sent to prison but to detention centres, where they await the finalization of the sentence. This process of 'finalization' can take many years, as legal representatives appeal for clemency. Miyazaki's initial death sentence was handed down on 14 April 1997. He later remarked that he found it difficult to find a comfortable sitting position as the judge delivered the sentence. He went on to complain that hanging, the method of execution favoured in Japan, was inhumane, and suggested the country move to the lethal injection method used in the United States.

For the next four years, Miyazaki was perfectly content, reading comic books all day in the detention centre whilst the wheels of justice slowly turned. He wrote hundreds of letters to the editor of his favourite magazine, *Tsukuru* ('Create'), which specializes in critiquing Japanese mass media and subcultures. In one such letter he commented on the fact that this death sentence was upheld by the Tokyo High Court in 2001: a court spectator shouted 'Drop dead now, bastard!' but Miyazaki only learnt of this afterwards as he had dozed off during the sentencing. What he also missed was Chief Justice Tokiyasu Fujita's opinion of him: 'The atrocious murder of four girls to satisfy his sexual desire leaves no room for leniency. The crime is cold-blooded and cruel'.

Despite this, Miyazaki remained convinced he would be acquitted, and expressed no remorse for his crimes. 'I don't intend to apologize,' he wrote in one of his letters.

Of his victims, he wrote: 'There's nothing much to say about them. I'm happy to think I did a good deed'. During the early period of his incarceration he had reason to be confident about his death sentence not being carried out: the justice minister, Seiken Sugiura, said that the death penalty went against his devout Buddhist beliefs, and no executions were carried out during his tenure. Even with previous, less peacable justice ministers at the helm, the average elapsed time between the finalization of a death sentence and the execution itself had been around eight years. All this changed, however, with the appointment of the ultra-conservative Kunio Hatoyama as justice minister in 2006.

The *Asahi* newspaper nicknamed him 'The Grim Reaper'. Hatoyama signed death warrants at a pace unprecedented in modern Japan, causing waves of panic amongst those on death row. Miyazaki sought help from the famous anti-death penalty activist Yoshihiro Yasuda, and ironically it was this that sealed his fate: the primary reason for a stay of execution was the argument that Miyazaki was insane, and his letter to Yasuda was seen as proof that he was of sound mind.

In Building A of the Tokyo Detention House in Tokyo's Kosuge district, the evening of 16 June 2008 was no different to any other for Miyazaki. In common with all Japanese death row convicts, he had no idea he would be hanged the next morning. The first indication a condemned man has that something is out of the ordinary is the sound of the guards' footsteps outside his cell. Miyazaki was offered a cigarette, Japanese confectionery, fruit and tea. He refused the offer of a prison chaplain to speak to until just before the moment of his execution. Then he was led into the execution room, divided in half by blue curtains. Facing him was a Buddhist statue, a cross and a rope 3 centimetres (1 inch) thick which was placed around his neck. He was blindfolded with a white cloth, and then three prison officials in a separate room simultaneously pushed a button to release the trapdoor. Only one button functions, so none of them can know for certain that they were responsible for snapping Miyazaki's neck. minutes later, a prison doctor in the room below climbed a stepladder and held a stethoscope to the serial killer's heart to confirm that he was dead.

As Miyazaki's body was being towelled down and dressed in white, the former deputy inspector of the Saitama prefectural police was back in the lonely woods of Kawagoe, west of Saitama. The 67-year old Sato Norimichi toured all of the sites of the crimes that day, offering up prayers to the four young victims of Japan's infamous killer. News of Miyazaki's death leaked to the media as he drove between the crime scenes. The story of the Otaku Killer was finally over.

CHAPTER FIVE

Robert William Pickton, 'The Pig Farmer Killer'

In March, 1997, bleeding heavily from multiple stab wounds, Wendy Lynn Eistetter staggered out of the Pickton Pig Farm and out on to the highway, still wearing a handcuff on one wrist. It was 1.45 am, so cars were few and far between, but she managed to flag down a motorist and collapse inside his car. The half-naked woman was rushed to the Eagle Ridge Hospital, where doctors managed to save her life. She told them that Robert 'Willy' Pickton was the man who had tried to kill her, after handcuffing her then stabbing her with a kitchen knife. She had wrestled the weapon off him, stabbed him with it and run for her life. Police arrested Pickton when he entered the same hospital to get his own wound treated. He was released on a $2,000 bond. Hospital staff used a key found in his pocket to release the handcuff from Wendy's wrist.

The police were already familiar with the Pickton brothers: five years earlier, in 1992, Willy's brother David had been convicted of sexual assault, and had committed numerous other minor offences. The Picktons bought their vehicles at the Vancouver police auctions. Willy was the 'slow' one, with a well below normal IQ of 86. He was considered a little strange, known to wear women's clothes and a wig, have muffins and ice cream for breakfast and eat all other food straight from the can. But he came across as a harmless eccentric rather than a man prone to violence. When Willy explained that it was Wendy who attacked him rather than the other way around, it was his word against hers. And Wendy's word didn't count for much with the Vancouver police: she was a drug addict and a prostitute known on the streets as 'Stich', and had a lengthy criminal record herself. 'The little bitch almost killed me', Pickton said; the deep slash to his neck could indeed have been fatal.

The Picktons certainly didn't seem unduly concerned by the gravity of the charges hanging over Willy: on New Year's Eve they threw one of their famous parties at 'The Piggy Palace', an after-hours club they ran on Burns Road, close to their land. Perhaps they already knew the charges would be dropped; they subsequently were in January 1998. Lead investigator Mike Connor said he felt it was a 'slam-dunk' but prosecutor Randi Connor decided a junkie like Wendy would never convince a jury. The police officer was sure that Pickton was a violent offender, and he sat in his car after midnight outside Pickton's farm on dozens of occasions, hoping he could catch him in the act. But after Connor was promoted in 1999 his surveillance of Pickton stopped. All the police files relating to the incident later mysteriously vanished. Pickton's clothing from that night sat in a Royal Canadian Mounted Police evidence locker until 2005, when it was eventually tested for DNA. It revealed traces of DNA from Cara Ellis and Andrea

Borhaven, two of the several women missing from the streets of Vancouver.

Downtown Eastside

One of the five women reported missing from Vancouver's Eastside neighbourhood in 1997 was Marnie Frey. Like many of those who had vanished, Marnie had been working the streets as a prostitute, and her absence was not immediately noticed. Though she hadn't been seen since 30 August, she wasn't reported as a missing person until 29 December. Her father Rick pounded the sidewalks of Downtown Eastside asking locals if they had any information. The prostitutes who worked there all told him the same harrowing tale: women were never seen again if they took rides out to the Pickton pig-farm. The Vancouver Rape Relief and Women's Shelter had heard the same rumours from their clients. But the police didn't seem to be acting on the information, and Marnie Frey remained Missing Persons Case #98-209922 for the rest of 1998.

In July that year, Coquitlam Police in British Columbia got a tip-off from Bill Hiscox, who worked for the Picktons' 'P&B Salvage Company' and occasionally visited their farm. He got chatting to a woman working as a cleaner there and she told him she had found bloody clothing and women's identification in Pickton's trailer. Bill contacted the police and Wayne Leng, who had left his phone number on posters in Downtown Eastside as part of his efforts to find his missing friend Sarah de Vries. She was a sex-worker well-known to the police, having recently turned up in a Port Moody police station half-naked and beaten black and blue. She recorded in her diary that they turned her back on to the streets without even offering her a blanket, so she hitchhiked home and was sexually assaulted en route. Her $1,000 a day heroin habit meant she couldn't be picky over punters, and she duly disappeared from her usual spot on the corner of Princess and Hastings. 'Just another Hastings Street whore/sentenced to death' she wrote in one of her numerous poems. Her white purse was later found in Pickton's loft, along with a used condom.

Despite Bill Hiscox's tip-off, the police failed to investigate Robert 'Willy' Pickton. Sarah was just one of 11 women who vanished without a trace that year.

Vancouver's Downtown Eastside is Canada's poorest district, home to many of the city's sex-workers, vagrants and drug-addicts. These are the people most vulnerable to a psychopathic predator, and Pickton had the easiest possible way to lure them in: everybody knew that you got a free fix of drugs out at the Piggy Palace, if you were willing to do whatever the Picktons asked.

The Piggy Palace

'Piggy' was Dave Pickton's nickname around Port Coquitlam, British Columbia. Willy would find fresh victims by prowling the so-called 'low track', the dozen or so alleyways and dark side streets of Eastside, where around 1,500 prostitutes sell their bodies. It was not illegal to do so in Canada in the 1990s, and nor was it illegal to pay for sex, but it was illegal to communicate for the purposes of prostitution or operate a brothel. Areas such as 'the low track' were the result: so-called 'Orange Light' areas, or Red Light areas where prostitution is tolerated. Willy had to work a little harder to find a girl who'd agree to head out with him along the dark highway to his squalid pig-farm but there was always someone who was desperate enough to do so. They call it 'survival sex work': what you do when you have no other options.

The farm was situated 30 kilometres (18 miles) or so east of Vancouver, behind a Save-On-Foods grocery store, a Costco and a Denny's restaurant. A sign at the entrance read: 'This property is protected by a pit bull with Aids'. It was known for wild parties at which the local Hell's Angels motorcycle gangs mixed with the likes of former mayor of Port Coquitlam, Scott Young. There was a rule to 'check your knives and other weapons in at the door' but other than that it was a place beyond the rule of law. The Picktons registered 'The Palace Good Times Society' with the government as a non-profit organization and built a dance hall that attracted crowds of up to 1,800 people before it was shut down in 2000 for failure to file financial statements.

The brothers had sold off much of their inherited farm-land to developers and no longer required an income: they had cash to burn, and that's what brought so many desperate visitors to the barns and trailers on their grim and forbid-ding farm. They kept 30 sheep, 12 pigs and a few goats, llamas and cows on the 11 hectares (27 acres) they still owned, but that was mostly because by law it was land that had to be farmed. The pigs may also have come in handy: they eat almost anything, including human remains. One associate of Pickton's later testified that he'd spoken of feeding dead prostitutes to pigs. Willie used to take the pig carcasses to the West Coast Reduction rendering plant on Commercial Drive North in Vancouver. It was right beside Downtown Eastside, the area so many women disappeared from. Willy was well known there as 'a bad date' – street slang for a punter who is violent to prostitutes.

So everyone knew Willy Pickton and the Piggy Palace, and everyone knew weird things happened out there. Everyone knew that young women were disappearing from the 'low track' of Vancouver's Downtown Eastside, too. It wasn't rocket science to work out that there might be a connection between the pig-farmer and the missing prostitutes. It didn't take a genius; though as it happened Vancouver Police had one.

Crunching numbers

In a seventh-floor room within the police station at 2120 Cambie Street, nicknamed 'The Officer's Mess', high-ranking police officers discussed the missing women over coffee. Detective Inspector Kim Rossmo wasn't allowed into the room – he was an outsider promoted from constable by then city chief Ray Canuel. At the time, Rossmo had become Canada's first police officer to graduate with a doctorate. He had earned a PhD in criminology at Simon Fraser University in British Columbia, where he developed geographic profiling, a computerized crime tool aimed at helping to catch serious repeat offenders, such as serial killers.

Rossmo studied the data of when missing people showed up and concluded that after three weeks 93 per cent were found. In Vancouver, however, the number found was close to zero. Rossmo's research also showed that no other city in Canada had experienced any similar phenomenon. In September 1998, Rossmo told a meeting of senior

Vancouver police officers the news they didn't want to hear: he believed a serial killer was on the loose, and he had already killed more than a dozen young women. Rossmo pleaded with them to warn the public of the situation in Vancouver. They argued that there was no concrete proof that such a killer was responsible for the women's disappearances. Many had transient lifestyles, they countered, and no stable jobs or accommodation. They'd turn up eventually.

Eventually they did – in tiny pieces, on Willy Pickton's pig-farm. He would later confess to murdering 49 women, one more than the 'Green River Killer' who was operating just across the border in the United States at around the same time. Despite the United States' reputation as home to more serial killers than any other country, it has yet to produce one with so high a body count as Canada's Robert 'Willy' Pickton – though tragically it would transpire that many of those 49 bodies would never be found.

By summer 1999, the pressure on the police was building. Public protests had raised awareness of the issue of the missing women, and a task force had been set up to look into the matter in the light of Kim Rossmo's geographic profiling data. With a $100,000 reward on offer for information, tip-offs began to pour in. One call to the Crime Stoppers hotline mentioned the name of Lynn Ellingsen, who had spent four months living in Willy Pickton's trailer from February to June that year. Enquiries confirmed that several people had claimed the 29-year-old recovering drug addict, Ellingsen, had told them the same horrific story about what she saw there.

The meat hook story

The story was that on 1 March, Ellingsen had been paid $150 by Pickton to help him pick up a prostitute. Even junkies desperate for a fix were wary of getting in a vehicle with Willy Pickton by this point, and having a female companion with him reassured them. It worked: Georgina Faith Papin hopped into his red pick-up truck, beside the smiling blonde woman who promised her a fun time. Georgina was 34, pretty and, like many of Pickton's victims, of aboriginal or 'First Nation' descent – Cree, in her case – she was proud of it, making traditional dreamcatchers and moccasins and baking bannock – the iconic Canadian bread that sustained the early settlers of this part of North America and remains a favourite of indigenous cultures even today. The granddaughter of baseball star Jimmy Rattlesnake, she'd had a tough upbringing in the foster-care system, run away at 12 and had the first of her seven children at the age of 14 in Las Vegas. She gave them Cree names: Winter Star, Little Storm, Autumn Wind. Like all those on the 'low track', Georgina had a long story to tell, but to Willy she was just another hooker, just another addict and just another victim.

Once she was at Pickton's farm, he handcuffed her, anally raped her and stabbed her to death. Ellingsen was in a different room so was unaware of the murder until she woke in the night and noticed the light was on in Willy Pickton's barn. When she investigated, she saw Georgina's body hanging from a meat hook, and Willy Pickton skinning her like a pig. He grabbed Ellingsen and pulled her into the barn, warning her that if she said anything then she would be hanging beside the dead woman. Ellingsen recalled seeing Georgina's painted red toe-nails dangling at her eye level, and described the yellowish colour of human fat when the skin has been removed. She told her horrified associates of how Georgina's bloody scalp, complete with the thick, lush, raven-coloured Cree hair, lay on a table nearby, 'like a horse tail'.

On 26 August, Constable Ruth Yurkiw of Vancouver police detachment and Detective Ron Lapine of the missing women's task force questioned Ellingsen about the story. She denied every word of it. With no first-hand account of anything criminal having taken place on the farm, Detective Earl Moulton was advised by a crown prosecutor that they had no grounds to seek a search warrant. It was only years later that Georgina's hands, which had so skilfully kneaded the dough of bannock bread, were found under a platform in Pickton's slaughterhouse. As for Lynn Ellingsen, she hooked up with an old boyfriend and got a job with a window company called 'See More Clearly'.

Brenda Ann Wolfe vanished from the low track on 5 March, just four days after Georgina Papin. She was a certified hairdresser, mother of two and a member of the Kahkewistahaw First Nation in Saskatchewan. Her DNA was later found on keys near handcuffs and legcuffs in the loft of Pickton's workshop.

In 2000, the police raided and shut down 'Grandma's House', the only place in Downtown Eastside that sex workers considered a safe space. The investigators continued to deny the rumours that a serial killer was on the loose.

Silence of an accomplice

Lynn Ellingsen would later claim she would have been afraid for her life had she told the police the truth about the Pickton pig-farm. Instead she kept quiet, and black-mailed Pickton in return for her silence while the list of missing women continued to grow: Andrea Borhaven was last seen in May 1999; Julie Young, in July; Wendy Crawford, in November; Jennifer Furminger, in December. At a New Year's Eve party in the Piggy Palace, a Royal Canadian Mounted Police radio room operative, Beverly Hyacinthe, saw Willy with a 'date', probably either Mona Wilson or Dawn Crey. She later recognized the date as a woman pictured on the front page of the Vancouver Province newspaper as a missing woman, but the information didn't reach the investigators. By then, Detective Inspector Kim Rossmo, the man who, back in 1998, had warned that a serial killer was at work, had left the force. He quit after his superiors demoted him back to the level of constable. In Washington, DC, they made him Director of Research at the elite Police Foundation.

Five years after the attack on Wendy Lynn Eistetter, Robert Willy Pickton remained a free man and the grim roll-call of victims continued: Yvonne Boen, last seen March 2001; Patricia Johnson, March; Heather Chinnock and Heather Bottomley, April; Angela Joesbury, June; Dianne Rock, October and Mona Wilson, November 2001.

Women continued to disappear from Downtown Eastside until February 2002, when a junior Royal Canadian Mounted Police Officer, who was not assigned to the case, got a tip-off. A former employee on the Pickton farm, Scott Chubb, claimed that illegal firearms were being stored on the farm. The Mountie decided to follow it up and he applied for a search warrant. On 5 February, he served that warrant on Willy Pickton, and began to look around his farm. He found more than illegal firearms. There was women's underwear, and an asthma inhaler, which matched the description of one belonging to Sereena Abotsway, one of the women listed as missing. It was enough for the police to start a more thorough search. That's when the Pickton farm finally yielded up its macabre secrets.

The palace of horrors

Mona Wilson's remains were amongst the first the police saw. She was 26, and known to her foster-mother Norma Garley as 'Running Bear', in honour of her aboriginal heritage. She'd told her foster family she was engaged to be married and had a good job, but in fact she'd worked the 'low track' of Downtown Eastside and been picked up by Willy. Her head, hands and feet had been stuffed into a bucket in the piggery. Her DNA was found on a dildo that had been attached to a .22-calibre revolver in Pickton's laundry room. It was also her blood that stained a foam mattress in a trailer on the farm.

The search widened and sure enough there were other buckets, other women. The remains of Sereena Abotsway and Andrea Joesbury were found next, their DNA mixed together. The women's heads had been cleaved in two and packed into buckets with their hands and feet. Sereena's Revenue Canada documents were found nearby in a rubbish bin, making her easier to identify. On 2 February 2002, Willy Pickton was charged with her first-degree murder, along with the murder of Mona Wilson. Both had been shot in the head. In the coming months, as more bodies were found and identified, their names were added to the list: Andrea Joesbury, Diane Rock, Jacqueline McDonell, Heather Bottomley, Brenda Wolfe, Georgina Papin, Helen Hallmark, Patricia Johnson, Jennifer Furminger, Heather Chinnock, Tanya Holyk, Sherry Irving and Inga Hall. As well as Marnie Frey, whose father, Rick, had been searching the streets of Vancouver for her. She was identified by from her jawbone recovered just outside the slaughterhouse.

A massive excavation of the entire Pickton farm ensued. It took years to complete, and cost an estimated $70 million. Rumours swirled around that Willy had fed human remains to his pigs and then sold the meat on the open market. Packages of ground meat containing the DNA of victims Inga Hall and Cindy Feliks were found on the farm. A publication ban was put in place to prevent the media from reporting some of the more salacious details of the case before it had gone to court. By the time of Pickton's trial the police believed they had found the remains, or DNA, of 33 women.

Emotionless on trial

Pickton's trial, which an earlier judge warned would be 'as bad as a horror movie', began at British Colombia Supreme Court on 22 January 2007. Crown prosecutor Derrill Prevett told the court that Pickton had confessed to killing 49 women and wanted to make it 'an even 50', but he 'got sloppy'. He was charged with 27 counts of first-degree murder. Defence lawyer Peter Ritchie urged the jury to keep an open mind about the case, which had caused a media sensation. Three hundred accredited journalists

Robert William Pickton

covered the trial for media outlets all over the world.

On 5–6 February, the videotape of a lengthy, secretly filmed conversation between Pickton and an undercover police officer planted in his jail cell after his arrest was shown in court. The section of Pickton masturbating in front of a security camera in the ceiling was edited out. He was heard to tell the undercover officer that the authorities were trying to 'bury' him. 'I'm screwed, tattooed, nailed to the cross, and now I'm a mass murderer', he said. The mass of those alleged murders was reduced by one in March when 'Jane Doe' was removed from the list of victims due to a lack of evidence. To avoid lengthening the trial unduly, the 26 remaining murders were split in two, and Pickton was charged with an initial six counts.

This splitting of the cases had a significant impact on the prosecution case: details pertaining to the 20 cases yet to be tried could not be submitted as evidence in the trial on the first six counts. So the jury never heard of Jennifer Lynn Furminger's DNA being found on an electric saw, of the various 'trophy' items of jewellery that Pickton kept, or of the used condoms with Pickton's DNA on them that were found in purses belonging to Dianne Rock and Sarah DeVries.

Much of the information they did hear was horrific enough, though. On 1 May, Justice James Williams called a short recess after some jurors became visibly shaken by the graphic evidence of forensic pathologist Dan Straathof relating to the autopsy of Mona Wilson's remains. On 25 June, Lynn Ellingsen told the story of how she had seen Georgina Papin's body hanging from a meat-hook; this time she was under oath. Forensic chemist Tony

Fung testified that he examined a syringe seized by police inside Pickton's trailer and determined it contained a diluted solution of methanol or methyl hydrate, better known as car windscreen washer fluid. Scott Chubb, the man who tipped off the police about Pickton, said Willy once told him a good way to kill someone would be to fill a syringe with windscreen washer fluid and inject them with it. Pickton showed no emotion, but scribbled copious notes as the 98 prosecution witnesses testified.

On 13 August, after seven months of harrowing testimony, the prosecution rested and the defence rose. They suggested people came and went all the time on the Pickton farm, and the man with the low IQ in the dock could not have killed so many and remained undetected for so long. Thirty witnesses testified that he was a decent, friendly, hard-working guy. Defence lawyers said the DNA evidence pointed more towards Pickton's friends being the culprits rather than the man himself. The jury began their deliberations on 30 November and returned with a verdict on 9 December.

They found him guilty on all six counts – not of first-degree murder but of second-degree: it appears they weren't convinced that he planned to kill, or that he acted alone. Despite the lack of a first-degree conviction, Pickton was sentenced to life in prison, with no possibility of parole for 25 years – the longest sentence then available under Canadian law. Since 2011 the law has changed, and consecutive parole ineligibility periods can be ordered for each murder. Justice James Williams called the crimes 'senseless and despicable' as he passed sentence.

Police officers stand guard outside the British Columbia Supreme Court on the first day of Robert Pickton's Trial, 22 January 2007.

Aftermath

It's impossible to know what aspects of the case weighed on the jury's deliberations, because it is illegal in Canada for jurors to speak about how they reached their verdicts. However, many of the relatives of the victims were convinced that the jury shared their own view on the case: others were involved. Some questioned why the police took so long to search the property, even going so far as to suggest that off-duty officers might somehow have been associated with Pickton. And then there were the two associates of Pickton who were arrested but never charged. The DNA of both Pat Casanova and Dinah Taylor was found at a variety of scenes on the farm, along with that of some of the missing women and several unidentified strangers. In total 235,398 samples were tested, yet to date only Willy Pickton has stood trial, and only for six murders. The other 20 counts that he faced were stayed on 4 August 2010.

The relatives claimed they were not kept informed of events relating to the case, nor offered any kind of support. Many struggled to find affordable accommodation to attend the ten-month trial, and were not entitled to financial assistance due to their 'Bill C-31' status. That's the controversial legislation that defines the rights of First Nation peoples, and the fact that so many victims came from an aboriginal background led to allegations that they were considered second-class citizens. The police vigorously deny that, but concede that only 53 per cent of murder cases involving aboriginal women are solved. They represent only 3 per cent of Canada's population, but from 2000–8 represented 10 per cent of female homicide victims in Canada.

After Pickton appealed his sentence and lost, the role of the Vancouver and Royal Canadian Mounted Police was examined by a special missing women commission of enquiry. The results were released in December 2012. Two successive Vancouver police chiefs, three deputy chiefs and other senior officers were severely criticized. Deputy Chief Constable Doug LePard of the Vancouver Police apologized to the victims' families, saying 'I would say to the families how sorry we all are for your losses and because we did not catch this monster sooner'. However, a recommendation by the enquiry commissioner Wally Oppal that the relatives be compensated by a 'healing fund' was rejected. The relatives had to sue in order to get any compensation: in March 2014 they were each awarded $50,000.

One other Canadian citizen who was unimpressed with the performance of the police was Dave Pickton, Willy's brother. In 2009, he sued them for damaging his property as they undertook their search. Those who knew the brothers always claimed that Dave was the dominant one, always telling Willy what to do, but he was never charged in connection with the crimes that happened on the farm they shared together, and nor was he called to testify at Willy's trial. He's thus a free man, and as far as the law is concerned, an innocent one. In 2012, he started the Pickton Foundation, a charity to help the poor in Ghana. But in the shelters and drop-in centres of Downtown Eastside, posters of a grinning Dave Pickton are pinned to the walls. 'BEWARE' reads the sign, with four exclamation points.

Every year since 2000, activists have organized a Memorial March through the streets of Vancouver on Valentine's Day to campaign for a public enquiry into the missing and murdered indigenous women of Canada, and to honour the lives of those who have died. In 2014, the Canadian government introduced Bill C-36, which made prostitution a criminal offence. Protesters who claimed it would make sex workers more vulnerable to predators dubbed the new legislation 'The Willy Pickton law'.

CHAPTER SIX

Andrei Chikatilo, 'The Rostov Ripper'

In June 1982, Major Mikhail Fetisov took charge of the crime scene near the small city of Novocherkassk, in the south-west of Russia. A body had been found by a man collecting firewood in the *lesopolosa*, a small strip of forested land planted near Soviet cities to prevent erosion. Military cadets ordered to conduct a search of the area turned up a sandal and bag that helped to identify the victim as 13-year-old Lyubov Biryuk. She'd been sent out to buy cigarettes for her father earlier the same month. They found the cigarettes in her bag untouched: the killer, most likely, did not smoke.

She had been stabbed repeatedly in a frenzied attack, which appeared to concentrate its ferocity on her eyes and her pelvic region. The summer that year had been warm and wet in Russia, and though Lyubov had been missing for only two weeks, her body was in an advanced state of decomposition. The Soviet forensic team, with their rudimentary techniques and equipment, would be of little help here.

Major Fetisov, the *syshchik* or lead detective with responsibility for the entire Rostov Oblast province, had seen nothing like it before. Murders in his area were either drunken attacks carried out by someone known to the victim or robberies in which the attacker wanted no witnesses. In this case, however, the killer appeared to be a perverse sexual thrill-seeker. Such criminals were thought to be the product of the decadent culture of the West, and were supposed to be unknown in the socialist utopia of the Soviet Union.

But in the coming months Major Fetisov would realize, with mounting horror, that this belief was wrong. He would be confronted with exactly the same scene of horrific brutality very soon. And the Soviet killer would go on to surpass even the most infamous killers in the West of whom the Major had read.

The 'Black Cat' prowls

The parents of missing ten-year-old Olga Stalmachenok received a macabre postcard with a chilling message: their daughter had been murdered and her body dumped in woods, and ten more victims would follow. Olga had gone missing on her way to piano lessons in Novoshakhtinsk, another small mining city in Rostov Oblast. The card was signed, in a shaky hand, 'Sadist Black Cat'.

It was 10 December and the Soviet people had buried their leader, Chairman Leonid Brezhnev, just a couple of weeks earlier. Yuri Andropov and Konstantin Chernenko would also die in office in quick succession before Mikhail Gorbachev became the last ever General Secretary of the Communist Party of the Soviet Union.

The police would be forced to conduct their hunt for the elusive serial killer in a country that was breaking apart around them.

By now three more bodies had been found, all with the same trademark mutilation of the eyes and sexual organs. There was little else to assist the investigators in finding the offender: none of the victims could even be identified. All appeared to be young females, but the lack of any coherent central database meant it was impossible for the bodies to be matched to persons who had been reported missing. In addition, the media was tightly controlled by the state, and information about crimes such as those committed by the 'Black Cat' was suppressed for fear of spreading panic and undermining morale. Soviet dictator Joseph Stalin had banned the disclosure of any crime data in 1933, and a succession of leaders since had suppressed any details that might cast the communist state in a bad light.

The children of Rostov began to look forward to the arrival of *Ded Moroz* ('Grandfather Frost'), the mythological figure who traditionally welcomed in the new year in the Soviet Union. Meanwhile, Major Fetisov and his team struggled desperately to protect them from an altogether more sinister figure. When the snows of winter finally thawed in April 1983, they revealed the mutilated body of Olga Stalmachenok.

1983: the year of suspicion

Major Fetisov recruited a lieutenant called Viktor Burakov from the criminology department to join his ever-expanding division of especially serious crimes. Burakov was a specialist in the analysis of physical evidence rather than a detective, but he would play a pivotal role in the investigation. He did not have many crimes to compare the current case against, but he possessed qualities that were rare in the Soviet police department of the time: the ability to keep an open mind, and a dogged determination to solve the case.

Burakov toiled through countless files on known sex offenders, previously released mental patients and men with prior convictions for violence in the Rostov area. As he did so, more bodies were discovered: those of a girl of 13 and a seven-year-old boy. A 45-year-old woman was also murdered, though police did not link that crime to the others – yet.

The seemingly isolated attack on a young boy was a puzzling turn of events, but the team did not have long to contemplate this outlier before they were faced with even more startling news. Burakov got a call to say that a man had confessed to all of the crimes. It appeared as though the long hunt was over.

Yuri Kalenik, a 19-year-old who had lived in a home for children with special needs, was arrested after a tip-off from one of his friends. He confessed after several days of interrogation, and agreed to take investigators to where he had hidden the bodies. Burakov tagged along, and was soon convinced that the suspect was not their man, much to his colleagues' displeasure. Kalenik struggled to point out the crime sites without prompting, and his confession contained no information that wasn't provided to him by the police. A new body was found in another wooded area that Kalenik apparently knew nothing of. She had been mutilated in much the same way as the others – in this case the victim's nipples had been removed, as well as the all-too-familiar damage done to the eyes. She'd been dead for several months, so Kalenik could still have been responsible, but Burakov thought otherwise.

The pressure from his superiors to charge the man and thus speedily resolve the Soviet Union's most troublesome murder case was immense. Burakov's reservations were soon shown to be well-founded, however: yet another body was discovered, this victim having been killed just three days earlier, whilst Kalenik was in custody. The killer was still out there.

What most horrified the investigators was that not only was the pace of the slaughter increasing, but the frenzy of violence against the victims was escalating, too. The latest body, found on 20 October, had been completely disembowelled, and her internal organs could not be located at the crime scene. Her eyes were, however, intact. The litany of unsolved murders was added to again when yet another body was discovered not far away. This woman had been dead for some months, having been killed over the summer.

In September, Soviet defence force Lieutenant Colonel Stanislav Petrov quietly saved the world from nuclear armageddon by ignoring an early warning system that indicated incoming nuclear missiles were about to strike the Soviet Union. He was later reprimanded by his superiors for improper filing of the paperwork relating to the incident. The investigation into the Rostov serial killer was characterized by a similar disconnect between those on the front line and the bureaucrats of the Communist Party system. The latter, for example, believed that homosexuality was a sexual perversion, and since the killer was also a sexual pervert he must, therefore, be a homosexual. Hundreds of man-hours were wasted raiding the homes of known or suspected homosexuals as a result. The moratorium on news stories relating to the murders continued, meaning children continued to wander the streets – oblivious to the danger and unprotected by their parents. They were easy prey. The inevitable result was that the murders continued.

A young boy from nearby Gukovo was reported missing on 27 December. His name was Sergei Markov. His body would not be found until Grandfather Frost had ushered in the New Year of 1984. This would, alas, be another bloody year in Rostov.

The dragnet

Sergei Markov had been struck from behind and then stabbed a total of 70 times. His genitals had then been hacked off and he had then been raped. It was an utterly horrific crime, and yet it offered the first real hope to the investigating officers. The body of Sergei had been preserved by the winter snows and yielded valuable clues. Most importantly, semen was found in his anus and a sample of it tested: it revealed that the subject's blood group was type AB. This could be compared against blood samples from suspects and, whilst the technology available could not provide a definitive match, it could eliminate suspects. That would prove important as the strong-arm interrogations of the Soviet police produced several false confessions in the course of the inquiry.

By September 1984, a total of 13 further bodies had been discovered in and around Rostov. All could be linked to the same man, and the hideous pattern of stabbing and mutilation was repeated at each crime scene. The killer had begun to cut off lips and noses, placing them in the mouths or slashed stomachs of his victims. Eight were under the age of 18, the youngest was just ten. Three were boys; the rest were female. In one instance a ten-year-old child had been killed at the same time as her 29-year-old mother.

The investigation floundered as the body count rose inexorably. Undercover officers were sent to patrol every train station in Rostov to observe suspicious behaviour. Female undercover officers flirted with strangers in order to try and bait the killer into striking. Inevitably, such a wide dragnet pulled in a vast number of suspects and potential leads. One of the thousands of men stopped and questioned was a 48-year-old man seen approaching a variety of adolescents and young women on Rostov's buses. He was found to be carrying a bag that contained a knife and some rope. As a result, he was arrested and brought in for further interrogation on 13 September 1984. His name was Andrei Chikatilo.

Comrade Chikatilo

Andrei Chikatilo was married, had two children and a steady job as a clerk in a Rostov factory.

He had completed his national service with an unblemished record, and joined the Communist Party in 1960. He had a degree in Russian literature and had previously worked as a teacher. A meek, mild-mannered, bespectacled man, he denied all knowledge of the killings in the local area. He informed his inquisitors that he was carrying a knife and rope because his work sometimes required him to use those items. He approached the young women on the buses because he used to work as a teacher and liked to converse with the young. His testimony appeared convincing.

But Comrade Chikatilo had a dark secret: he had been forced to quit a variety of teaching jobs after being accused of sexually assaulting his pupils. He was also under investigation for theft from a previous employer. He had already been arrested and questioned about the murder of a nine-year-old girl in 1978. Another man had been found guilty of that crime and executed for it. Still, Chikatilo raised enough suspicion for a blood sample to be taken. It came back as type A. The semen samples recovered from the victims of the killer were all type AB. He could not be their man.

Chikatilo was tried and sentenced to a year in prison for the thefts from his employer. He was no longer considered a suspect in the Rostov murders, due to the lack of a match from his blood sample. The investigators had just made a catastrophic mistake.

Killer X

Chikatilo was released in December 1984, and found a new job at a locomotive factory in the city of Novocherkassk. During his period of incarceration, the team investigating the Rostov murders had been puzzled at the sudden absence of new victims. No further bodies would turn up until the middle of the following year. A bulletin was sent out to all other forces in the Soviet Union describing the suspect's killing pattern, in case he had moved away from the Rostov area. No response was forthcoming. Two bodies found around Tashkent (in what is modern-day Uzbekistan but

Andrei Chikatilo

was then part of the Soviet Union's southern border with Afghanistan) were checked but dismissed. One had been beheaded, and the injuries on the body of the other one were so extensive that the authorities believed they must have been the result of an accident with a harvesting machine. It was another blunder. Before his arrest in Rostov, Chikatilo had flown to Tashkent for a business meeting.

Investigators Fetisov and Burakov decided to try an approach that was unprecedented in the history of Soviet crime detection: they would bring in a psychologist to build a profile of the offender. The man they turned to was Dr Alexandr Bukhanovsky from Moscow, whose specialist subject was homosexuality and transsexuality. It was the closest subject area that they could find, and he was one of the few psychiatric experts willing to risk his reputation on such a bizarre and difficult case. He produced a 65-page report on the suspect, whom he termed 'Killer X'.

Nobody in the Soviet Union at this time much trusted psychological profiling: it smacked too much of the bourgeois world-view of the West. But the investigators did at least take on board one of the key predictions made by Dr Bukhanovsky: the killer was heterosexual, and suffering from some kind of sexual dysfunction. He needed to watch a person die in order to achieve sexual gratification. Removing the genitals of his male victims was a way of turning them into surrogate females, which were the people he most desired. As a result of this insight, the investigators turned their attention away from Rostov's homosexual population. They soon found that another Dr Bukhanovsky's predictions was also accurate: the killer would only ever stop temporarily, if he thought he was in danger of immediate capture. As soon as he felt safe, he would kill again. And so it proved.

A body found in a thicket of woods close to Domodedovo Airport, Moscow, in August 1985 displayed strikingly similar injuries to the Rostov cases. When Burakov flew in to check the crime out, he was convinced that his killer was responsible. He laboured to check all of the hand-written tickets to find anyone who had flown between Rostov and Moscow in late July. No names of interest were found. Three more bodies were discovered, but they were boys, and investigators did not link them to the crimes in Rostov.

And so Andrei Chikatilo travelled back from Moscow to Rostov the same way he had arrived – by train.

Desperate measures

Lead investigator Viktor Burakov was by now a desperate man. He had been pursuing the killer for over three years, had chased down thousands of leads and interviewed dozens of suspects, but the body count continued to rise. Now the killer had moved to the capital. The pressure on Burakov to find the man who was terrorizing the Soviet Union was immense. In a wooded area near the Shakhty bus depot 75 kilometres (46 miles) north-east of Rostov-on-Don was yet another murdered teenager, her mouth stuffed with leaves, unquestionably the victim of the same remorseless killer.

But the killings then suddenly stopped. No more bodies were found for the rest of 1985, and the eerie silence from the killer continued throughout 1986. Any relief felt by Burakov was tempered by the frustration of having no new crime scenes, and thus no new clues. He was by now at a total loss as to how to proceed. With no new information an no one else to seek advice from, Burakov turned to an unlikely figure for help: Anatoly Slivko. He was not a psychologist, detective or forensics expert. He was a serial killer, sitting on death row awaiting execution.

Slivko had stalked his victims in Nevinnomyssk, Stavropol Krai, which bordered Rostov Oblast. He had murdered seven boys between 1964 and 1985. His preferred method of murder had been to persuade his victims to partake in an 'experiment' involving hanging them until they were unconscious, in order, he said, to stretch their spines. He hanged a total of 43 boys, many of whom were sexually assaulted once they were unconscious. The fact that he let some of his victims escape with their lives eventually led to his arrest. Chikatilo never made that mistake, and so the interview with Slivko did not provide Burakov with any fresh insights.

Slivko was executed just hours later. Burakov suffered a nervous breakdown shortly afterwards. He spent a month in hospital. But upon his release he immediately returned to work on the Chikatilo case.

No more bodies were discovered for the rest of 1986, or throughout 1987, as Burakov pored over his notes and chased down new leads. Eventually, on 16 April 1988, came evidence that the killer had struck again. The body of a young woman was found near railway tracks at Krasny Sulin, stabbed and mutilated but not sexually assaulted. A month later the body of a nine-year old boy was found in woods near a train station in the Ukrainian city of Ilovaisk.

He had suffered numerous knife wounds, had been castrated, sodomized and then had dirt stuffed into his orifices. The killer had become active again.

The weeks dragged by, and more bodies were found, despite the undercover police presence at key stations. An eight-year-old boy's body was discovered beside a road, leading some to suspect that the police were wasting their time in monitoring public transport hotspots. The body of a Hungarian student was next to be found, in a wooded area far from any bus or train station. The remorselessly rising body count continued into 1990, reaching a total of 32 victims. The public, now increasingly aware of the crimes, became outraged at the apparent inability of the police to protect them. The Soviet authorities were nervous of any mass protest at this time: it was a period later called 'The Autumn of Nations', in which non-violent revolution had brought a non-communist leader to power in the Soviet satellite state of Poland. Similar revolutions were already in progress in Hungary, East Germany, Bulgaria, Czechoslovakia and Romania. The Iron Curtain of the Warsaw Pact countries was being torn apart.

Closing in on the killer

Much had changed inside the Soviet Union, too, during the seven years that the authorities had been chasing the Rostov killer. It was now 1989, two years since General Secretary Mikhail Gorbachev announced that under the Soviet policy of *glasnost* ('publicity' or 'transparency') no subject would be off limits for the media. At last, the press could begin to report the savage crimes in the Rostov area. With this social change came a new plan in the hunt for the Rostov killer.

Burakov wanted all of the Soviet Union to know about his latest operation, which involved flooding train and bus stations with uniformed officers. The intention was to make it impossible for the killer to operate in the entire central Rostov area. The police would deliberately leave a few more remote stations unguarded, in the hope that the killer would be lured out to them. The lonely station at Donleskhoz was selected as one target station, since the killer had struck there before. At these secret target stations, dozens of undercover police would pose as everyday rail passengers. If the killer emerged, they would swoop in and arrest him. But before the plan could be put into effect, however, the killer struck again – at the very location identified as the police's 'honey pot', Donleskhoz Station.

It was a hugely expensive operation, and deliberately high profile, so Burakov was staking his entire career on the plan's success. Having drawn so much attention to the case, he was under more pressure than ever to solve it. The weeks dragged by, and the killer managed to strike again, somehow slipping through the dragnet. But Burakov held his nerve, and the operation continued. Finally, on 6 November 1990, the man the police had been hunting for eight years approached a young woman right in the centre of the elaborate police trap – at Donleskhoz Station. Her body was found in nearby woods a week later. No one had seen a thing.

Svetlana Korostik, known at first to police only as 'Victim 36', was 22 years old. She had been beaten and sliced open, and part of her tongue had been cut off. Although the undercover officers at Donleskhoz had inexplicably failed to prevent her murder, one of them did observe a suspicious man emerging from the woodland where her body was found. He questioned the man and asked to see his papers. Since they were in order, he allowed the man to go and filed a routine report on the incident. However, when Burakov crosschecked the report against the names he had on file, it came back as a match: it was Andrei Chikatilo.

Nine grams

Chikatilo was arrested on 20 November 1990. Under intense interrogation over a period of nine days, he denied everything. With only a day left to charge or release him, the investigators knew they had only circumstantial evidence and, worse still, tests confirmed that Chikatilo was blood group A, and the semen found at many of the crime scenes was AB. It seemed the man they had now arrested on three separate occasions would have to be released once again.

Burakov turned to psychiatric expert Dr Bukhanovsky, who read Chikatilo the report he had written on 'Killer X'. The effect of hearing himself described so accurately and so calmly was extraordinary. Chikatilo broke down and admitted his crimes. Within hours, he was providing a detailed confession to 34 of the 36 murders to which the police had linked him. In addition, he confessed to many more of which the police were unaware, dating back to 1978.

The Soviet Flag was lowered from the Kremlin for the last time just a year after Chikatilo's arrest. The serial killer was charged with 53 murders by the fledgling Russian

Federation – and was found guilty in 52 of the cases. On the 15th of October, 1992, Judge Leonid Akubzhanov made the following pronouncement:

"Taking into consideration the horrible misdeeds of which he is guilty, this court has no alternative but to impose the only sentence that he deserves. I therefore sentence him to death."

The death sentence was known colloquially in the Soviet era as *devyat gram*, which means nine grams (0.3 ounces) in Russian, the weight of the 7.62 mm bullet used to shoot the condemned person in the back of the head. Chikatilo kicked his bench across the cage when he heard the verdict, and began shouting abuse. He was executed on the 14th of February, 1994.

Holodomor's children

Chikatilo's trial shed some light on what motivated him to commit such terrible crimes, but inevitably fell short in terms of fully answering the question of why such a seemingly normal man could turn into 'The Rostov Ripper'.

The primary source of Chikatilo's murderous frustration was his inability to perform sexually. In the West, today, this can be easily treated. But Chikatilo was born in 1936, in the Ukrainian Soviet Socialist Republic, a place and a period that would define the dark trajectory of his life. He described himself in his court testimony as 'a poisoned wolf', and the poison that paralyzed his moral sensibilities came indirectly from two of the century's most tyrannical dictators, Stalin and Hitler.

Stalin's plan to modernize the Soviet Union required

Chikatilo on trial in 1992

machinery and technology from the West, and in the 1930s the only way to pay for this was by exporting grain. In Ukraine, in particular, little was left for the general population and famine was widespread. Millions died in the ensuing *Holodomor* ('Hunger extermination'). Survivors were driven to cannibalism, and Chikatilo's mother claimed that his older brother had been among those eaten. This may go some way towards explaining his later compulsion to tear body parts off with his teeth and consume the flesh of his victims. Ukraine was still recovering from the horror of *Holodomor* just as Hitler's 'Master Race' invaded in 1941. More famine and brutality followed, and during Chikatilo's formative years his father was absent, held in a Nazi prisoner of war camp.

Chikatilo stated at his trial that it was this upbringing that turned him into a serial killer. But terrible though his childhood undoubtedly was, millions of others suffered similar torments without going on to murder innocent strangers. Judge Leonid Akubzhanov asked time and again what drove Chikatilo to commit the crimes, but he could only mumble 'I can't explain'. He once told investigators 'I began to wonder whether these low-class elements have the right to exist'. At his trial he made the exact same judgement upon himself: 'I know I have to be destroyed,' he said. 'I understand. I was a mistake of nature.' The prosecution agreed – even explaining away the mistakes they made in their own blood-test labs by suggesting that Chikatilo, uniquely, had separate A and AB types for his blood and semen.

In the end, Chikatilo's actions defy rational explanation. The communist system that first fostered him and then hunted him remains equally difficult to understand. Indeed, it was the paranoid secrecy of that system that allowed Chikatilo to commit crimes that went undetected for so long. Children were taught that all Soviets were part of the same communist family. There were no strangers or dangers in the red utopia of the Soviet Union, and parents were never warned that a killer was on the loose. Chikatilo boasted of how easy it was to snatch unwary, trusting children and drifters and lead them to their doom: 'I'd just say to all of them, 'Let's go, let's have something to eat,' or whatever. They were everywhere, at every step. I didn't have to search for them'.

CHAPTER SEVEN

John Reginald Christie, 'The Rillington Strangler'

Whilst the airwaves crackled with reports of the Allied advance into Nazi Germany in 1944, a delivery driver at the Ultra Electric Limited radio factory walked back to his lodgings at 10 Rillington Place in West London. By his side was his 32-year-old co-worker Muriel Amelia Eady. Muriel was suffering from bronchitis and John Reginald Christie had spoken of a 'special mixture' he had created that could cure her cough. The two were friends, having gone out as a foursome with Christie's wife and Muriel's steady boyfriend. But Christie's wife was visiting relatives in Sheffield when he took Muriel into his small, grimy kitchen and sat her on a chair. There, after a quick cup of tea, he instructed her to inhale a mixture of Friar's Balsam, a popular pungent cold cure, from a jar. As she did so, he slipped behind her and connected a second tube in the jar, which led to the gas supply of his cooker. Within moments Muriel was unconscious from the carbon monoxide it contained.

Christie then raped her, whilst strangling her with a stocking. He would later bury her in his tiny back garden, next to the woman he had murdered a year earlier. Whilst digging the grave he disturbed his earlier victim's bones: he used her decomposed femur to prop up a trellis fence that was in danger of collapsing.

Fascination with death

Born to an authoritarian father and a mother who was overprotective of him, Christie was often bullied by his four older sisters. His grandfather was austere and severe, and when he died, the eight-year-old Christie experienced pleasure at seeing the corpse laid out for the wake. He began to play alone in the nearby graveyard, peeking with fascination into the crumbling vaults that housed the coffins. A lifelong fascination with death had begun. It is one that has eerie parallels with another British serial killer, Dennis Nilsen, who killed six people in North London in the 1970s and 1980s. He, too, saw his grandfather's body laid out for a wake and claimed to be forever changed by the experience.

Sex and violence

The lonely Christie grew into a frustrated teenager who could not perform sexually with women, earning him the nickname 'Reggie-No-Dick' amongst his peers. He asserted his masculinity by signing up for the army at the outbreak of the First World War, but suffered serious injuries during a mustard gas attack. He was left blind for several months, and unable to speak. It is unclear if the damage caused to Christie's health was primarily physical or psychological, but for the rest of his life he spoke in a low voice that many found difficult to hear or understand.

The year after the war ended, Christie married a woman by the name of Ethel Simpson, and found work as a postman in Ethel's home town of Sheffield. The marriage was blighted by Christie's sexual problems, and his work-life was little better: he was soon fired after being caught stealing letters. He was sentenced to three months in prison and on release struggled to find another job. His prospects, he decided, would be better in London. Ethel remained with her family in Sheffield.

Christie had began using prostitutes early on in his youth, and continued to do so when he arrived in London – which had a plentiful supply. His run-ins with the law continued over the next few years and gradually his crimes became more serious and more violent. In 1923, he was bound over for obtaining money on false pretences, and given 12 months' probation for violent conduct. The following year he received a total of nine months' imprisonment for larceny. By 1929, he was serving six months' hard labour in Wandsworth Prison for assaulting a woman with whom he was living in Battersea, South London. That incident could have been a lot worse: in what the judge described as 'a murderous attack' Christie had struck Maud Cole on the head with a heavy wooden cricket bat. Many reports describe Cole as a prostitute, but there is no evidence for this. There is also no evidence that she was aware that the man she was living with had a wife in Sheffield.

Christie was behind bars again in 1933 after stealing a Morris Oxford car (many reports claim it belonged to a priest who had given the ex-con a second chance, but this appears to be an exaggeration created later by the media).

Some time after being released from prison he managed to persuade his wife to abandon her job as a typist in Sheffield and join him in London.

In 1937, the newly reconciled couple moved into a flat in a street of three-storey brick terraced houses close to the Metropolitan line of The London Underground train station. The house was divided into three separate flats, which shared a single outside lavatory. The Christies soon moved from the top-floor flat to the ground floor, where they had access to a tiny garden: a huge plus, as Reginald enjoyed gardening, and it gave an outside space for the family dog and cat.

The address was 10 Rillington Place of Notting Hill, London. It would shortly become synonymous in Britain with the most shocking acts of murder.

Notting Hill

Today, Notting Hill is a fashionable, well-to-do area of West London, immortalized by the romantic comedy film of the same name, and famously home at one time to ex British prime minister David Cameron. But it wasn't always so. When Christie moved there from his birthplace in Halifax, Yorkshire, in 1938, it was a down-at-heel area of cheap multi-occupancy lodgings, popular with immigrant communities for its low rents. He had moved to London to start his life anew after his criminal past in the North of England caught up with him. In the 1950s, Notting Hill would become synonymous with the slum landlord Peter Rachman, who made a fortune from cramming large numbers of tenants into substandard accommodation, but in Christie's first few years in London the immediate danger

A body being removed from 10 Rillington Place, 1953.

was not poverty, but bombs. The nearby All Saints' Church was just one of many buildings destroyed when the Luftwaffe blitzed the streets throughout the summer of 1940.

The Rillington years

At the outbreak of the Second World War, Christie joined the War Reserve Police. He would normally have been ineligible to do so due to his criminal record, but there was a war on, and it appears nobody did a background check on him. Around 17,000 such 'special constables' were recruited during the war and despite their minimal training, they enjoyed full police powers. Their role was primarily to patrol the blackouts that were enforced during German air raids, assist with evacuations and rescue those trapped in the rubble left by Hitler's bombers. Operating out of Harrow Road Police Station, Christie was in his element: always a pompous and officious man, he now had considerable power over his neighbours and enjoyed bossing them around. It also gave him a certain level of impunity with regard to committing crimes of his own.

He continued to visit prostitutes, and began an affair with a married woman whose husband was serving overseas. In 1943, the man in question returned home and beat Christie up after discovering the affair. One of the many women that Christie met with was a 21-year-old Austrian called Ruth Fuerst, who during the day worked in a munitions factory. She is usually referred to as a part-time prostitute, and it is possible this is true, but it may be that she was hoping to trade sexual favours with Christie in return for him turning a blind eye to some other aspect of her behaviour. Whatever the truth, in August 1943 she accompanied Christie back to Rillington Place, where they had sex. During the act, Christie suddenly grabbed her by the throat and strangled her. When he pulled himself out from inside her, urine and excrement cascaded out of her body on to the bed.

Christie threw out the sheets, then lifted the floorboards of his front living room and hid the body underneath them. Ethel and her brother came home and the three of them had tea together, only one of them aware of the corpse beneath their feet.

The next day, Christie took up the floorboards again and dragged the body out to the washhouse, where he left it while he dug a hole in the garden. The process took some time, and Reginald took a break from his exertions to have tea with his wife when she returned from work. Once she went to bed, he finished his 'gardening' and buried the body, raking everything tidy the next morning.

New neighbours

On Easter Monday 1948, the Christies were joined at 10 Rillington Place by a pair of young newlyweds who were expecting their first child. Timothy and Beryl Evans took the top-floor flat, where their violent arguments frequently echoed through the entire street. Usually the disagreements were about money: Beryl was just 19 and enjoyed pampering herself and Timothy's meagre van driver's wages rarely allowed her to do so, particularly given her husband's thirst for beer. At times the exchanges became physical – both had violent tempers, and Beryl confided to Ethel that on one occasion Timothy had tried to strangle her.

When Beryl announced she was pregnant with their second child early in 1949, they both agreed that they could barely afford to raise their daughter Geraldine, let alone another child, and that the best option would be an abortion. That was a problem in England at this time, as the Offences Against The Person Act of 1861 outlawed such procedures under threat of a maximum penalty of life imprisonment. Beryl tried taking overdoses of pills, but that didn't work. John Christie offered to help. Christie told the couple that he had medical training and could abort the unwanted foetus, having performed similar operations successfully several times before. It was a lie, but they trusted the former war reserve policeman and were desperate enough to accept his offer. While Charles Kitchener, the second-floor tenant, was in hospital the middle flat of the house was empty for a period of about five weeks, and it was in his kitchen that the procedure would take place.

Exactly what happened next would be debated in English courts on several occasions, and remains highly contentious to this day. What is beyond dispute is that Beryl Evans, and her baby daughter Geraldine, were both strangled and then wrapped in a tablecloth in the washhouse of 10 Rillington Place. Timothy Evans later walked into a police station claiming he had killed his wife and disposed of her body down a drain. The British police immediately conducted a search of the property, but left without noticing anything incriminating. No small feat, given the presence of two bodies in the washhouse, two more in the back garden and a human thigh-bone propping up the garden fence.

A marginally more thorough search on 2 December at least uncovered the two bodies in the washhouse. Evans was put on trial for murder, though he now changed his story and claimed that his neighbour John Reginald Christie had killed his wife and child. Christie was the prosecution's chief witness at the trial, denying all knowledge of the crimes and testifying that Evans was an aggressive man who had been violent towards his wife in the past. The trial lasted for only three days and the jury took just 40 minutes to find Evans guilty of murdering his daughter; he was charged, but not tried, for the murder of his wife. He was hanged on 9 March 1950, dispatched by the celebrated British executioner Albert Pierrepoint, who had recently arrived back in the country after hanging 202 Nazi war criminals in Germany.

Evans had no prior criminal record for violence, only one for theft. As he swung on the end of Pierrepoint's rope, Ruth Fuerst's thigh-bone still propped up the garden fence of 10 Rillington Place, unnoticed by police. Children played with Muriel Eady's skull in a bomb crater nearby. Christie's dog had dug it up, so he had chucked it in a handy blitzed terrace on his way to work. London at the time was still full of bomb-sites, still full of bones, so when the kids handed it to the Notting Hill police station the policemen paid no attention to it. The bodies in Christie's garden remained undiscovered. Had the jury known of them, perhaps they would not have convicted Evans. And perhaps the slaughter of young women would have ended there. But it was not to be.

Mrs Christie

New tenants moved into the top-floor flat at Rillington Place and this caused friction with the Christies. The newcomers were West Indian immigrants, from Jamaica; like many white English working-class couples, the Christies considered themselvers to be culturally superior to the newcomers. The old British Empire had been transformed into a Commonwealth of Nations, of which Jamaica was a member. Britain was desperate to encourage immigration to help rebuild the shattered country after the devastation of the Second World War. The 'Windrush generation' of African-Caribbean men and women began to arrive in the passenger ship of that name in 1948 and tens of thousands more soon followed. Many ended up in West London, and Notting Hill would become the scene of race riots by 1958. In a microcosm of such tensions, Ethel prosecuted one of her new neighbours for assault, and via legal mediation the Christies negotiated exclusive use of the back garden.

The stress took its toll on Christie. He'd lost his job after the Evans trial revealed his criminal past, and now he added depression to his long list of ailments: a profound hypochondriac since childhood, he visited doctors on 173 separate occasions over the course of 15 years. He saw a psychiatrist and was hospitalized for three weeks. Ethel was growing more and more frustrated with him, and with the two of them at home all day the frequency and intensity of their arguments increased. Ethel retired to bed early on 12 December and Christie quietly slipped in beside her, then strangled her with a ligature. He dragged her body into the parlour and hid it beneath the floorboards there, wrapped in a flannel blanket and silk nightgown.

Christie alone

As Christmas 1952 approached, Christie's more friendly neighbours began to ask him where his wife was. He told them she was away up north, visiting her relatives. When her relatives in Sheffield later wrote asking why she hadn't been in touch over the Christmas period, Christie wrote back saying Ethel's rheumatism was preventing her from holding a pen. Suspicion gradually grew, as when the chatty Ethel was last seen taking the washing to Maxwell Laundries she had mentioned nothing about an extended trip to Sheffield. Christie sold Ethel's wedding ring and watch, then forged her signature to empty her bank account. With no wages coming in, he was desperate for money, and soon sold all of the furniture in the house and took to sleeping on a mattress on the floor. One item he kept hold of was the chair in the kitchen: he needed that for his 'operations'. He now had the ground-floor flat to himself, and could invite whomever he pleased back there, whenever he liked.

On 12 January 1953, Rita Nelson discovered she was pregnant again. The 25-year-old blonde prostitute met Reginald Christie in a local pub soon after, and he offered to help her with her 'problem'. It was her landlady that reported her as missing. Christie would later claim she attacked him with a frying-pan and he strangled her in self-defence, but the autopsy showed she suffered the same fate as Muriel Eady: gassed and strangled. He left the body where it was, made himself a cup of tea and then went upstairs to sleep on the mattress. The next morning he wrapped the body up and diapered it with a piece of material. With Ethel still under the floorboards and two

John Reginald Christie

women buried in the back garden, he was running out of space in the small flat. He found a small alcove behind a cupboard in the kitchen, and squeezed the body in there.

Later the same month, whilst having a cup of tea in a Notting Hill café, Christie overheard another prostitute associate of his discussing her search for accommodation. He invited 26-year-old Kathleen Maloney to look at the flat above his. She was never heard from again. Like the others, she was gassed and strangled, then raped. He diapered her corpse and left her propped up dead on the kitchen chair until the next morning. Then he made himself breakfast and a cup of tea before making room for her body in the same alcove as he had hidden that of Rita Nelson. He had to place her legs vertically against the back wall in order to get the door of the alcove cupboard shut.

Hectorina McLennan was the next to be shown around Rillington Place, but she showed up for the house inspection with her boyfriend in tow, which was not what Christie had planned. The 26-year-old and her partner ended up moving in, despite the lack of furniture, and stayed for several nights before Christie changed his mind and asked them to leave. Before they could do so, Christie got Hectorina drunk, gassed her, throttled her and raped her. By now it was getting almost impossible to squeeze more bodies into the alcove cupboard, but Christie eventually managed it by placing Hectorina in a sitting position and tying her bra to the blanket that he'd wrapped around Kathleen Maloney's legs. Inevitably Hectorina's boyfriend came around in search of her, and Christie calmly made him a cup of tea whilst they discussed her mysterious disappearance.

On the run

With a total of five bodies in 10 Rillington Place, Christie must have realized that his situation was untenable, and that he would have to move on. He rented out the flat, had his dog put down and on 20th of March 1953, he took to the streets. The next day the unfortunate tenants who had taken over the Rillington Place address learned that Christie didn't own it, and the real landlord Charles Brown asked them to leave. By then Christie was staying in Rowton House in King's Cross, then another run-down part of London. Rowton House consisted of a chain of hostels designed to house working men who would otherwise find themselves on the streets or in squalid lodging houses. As Christie aimlessly walked the streets of London, his landlord sought new tenants for Rillington Place, and gave permission for the existing top-floor tenant to use the facilities of the flat downstairs.

This top-floor tenant, Jamaican jazz musician Beresford Dubois Brown, decided to clean up the foul-smelling kitchen, and in doing so stumbled across the three bodies packed into the kitchen alcove cupboard. Horrified, he called the police. They immediately began a search for the former resident at the property, John Reginald Christie. His picture was plastered over the front page of every newspaper in the country. Christie then left his King's Cross hostel after staying for just four of the seven nights he had booked, and swapped his distinctive rain coat for one worn by another man. For the next few days he slept on park benches and in cinemas, constantly on the move in an attempt to avoid detection. But on the last day of March 1953, a police constable spotted the dishevelled figure on Putney Embankment, beside the River Thames. After Christie gave him a false name and address, the constable asked him to remove his hat. The huge gleaming forehead was highly distinctive and the officer recognized at once that this was the man whose picture had been in the papers. Christie was arrested and taken to Putney Police station.

On trial – mad or wicked?

I his trial on the 22nd of June 1953, defence lawyer Derek Curtis-Bennett QC described his client in court as 'as mad as a March hare', and Christie pleaded not guilty to murder on the grounds of insanity. Why, Curtis-Bennett argued, would Christie kill not only all of these women but also his wife Ethel, 'the one person he liked'? He was 'an object of pity rather than of horror'. But Attorney-General Sir Lionel Heald QC, acting for the prosecution, poured scorn on this notion and sought to reveal a dangerous sexual predator hiding beneath the veneer of a harmless bespectacled middle-aged loner. In his summing-up, Mr Justice Finnemore said: 'The mere fact that a man acts like a monster, cruelly and wickedly, is not of itself evidence that he is insane ... I do not know whether any jury before in this country or perhaps in the world has seen and heard a man charged with murder go into the witness box and say, 'Yes I did kill this victim, I killed six others as well over a period of ten years'.

One hour and 26 minutes after the jury had retired from No 1 Court to consider its verdict, a black cap was laid on Mr Justice Finnemore's head, according to the tradition in Britain when a death sentence was passed. He has hanged on the 15th of July 1953. The hangman Albert Pierrepoint later recalled: 'I hanged John Reginald Christie, the Monster of Rillington Place, in less time than it took the ash to fall off a cigar I had left half-smoked in my room at Pentonville'.

Capital punishment in Britain

The case of the other man hanged by Pierrepoint, Timothy Evans, now took centre stage in the story. Two enquiries were held and two parliamentary debates undertaken in order to establish whether an innocent man had been sent to the gallows. Evans had accused Christie of the murder of his wife, and Christie had confessed to that crime – but Christie never confessed to killing baby Geraldine, and that was the crime for which Evans was hanged. An initial report concluded that Evans was guilty of both murders, then a later one concluded he had not committed the crime for which he was tried – killing his daughter – and he was granted a posthumous pardon in 1966. At the High Court in 2004, judges accepted that Evans had not killed either his wife or his child, but refused formally to quash his conviction on the grounds of cost.

The case of Timothy Evans was a major factor in shifting public opinion in Britain away from supporting the death penalty for murder. His execution scarred the collective conscience of the nation, in part because of its association with the horror of John Reginald Christie. Just four years after Christie's trial, the Homicide Act removed the automatic death penalty for all murders, though any murder committed for theft was still likely to see a convict hang. In 1965, the House of Commons passed a bill to abolish the death penalty for murder (you could still be hanged for 'high crimes', such as treason or espionage, until 1998, though no one actually was).

London is infamous as the city that was stalked by perhaps the most notorious serial killer of all time, Jack the Ripper, but after that Victorian monster disappeared from its streets very few similar criminals followed in his footsteps. John Christie was cut from a very different cloth to the bragging demonic Jack. He redefined for the British, and the world, what a serial killer looked like. Jack gave us the image of a cloaked figure darting through darkened alleyways after slashing the throats of ladies of the night. Christie was balding, bespectacled and lived in a terraced house: he looked like most people's neighbours. He was an ex-policeman, whose quiet, well-spoken words were so convincing they sent an innocent man to the gallows for the crimes he himself had committed. Even the monstrous Moors Murderers, the Yorkshire Ripper, Harold Shipman and Fred and Rosemary West would go to prison rather than the gallows. They had Christie to thank for that – though many believe a life sentence to be the harsher fate. Both Shipman and Fred West chose to hang themselves rather languish in a cell for the rest of their days.

CHAPTER EIGHT

Moses Sithole, 'The ABC Killer'

On Sunday 18 December 1994, word began to spread through the South African township of Atteridgeville that police had shot 'The Cleveland Strangler'. The man, who had already confessed to murdering 15 women in a suburb of Johannesburg, was also the prime suspect in the investigation to find 'The Atteridgeville Strangler', who was believed to be responsible for several murders in the Pretoria area. Soon the same man was linked to an attack in Boksburg. He was soon dubbed 'The ABC Killer' by local media as he had begun his career of violence in Atteridgeville, moved on to Boksburg and was finally arrested in Cleveland.

The suspect had agreed to guide police to the spot where he had left the body of one of his victims. His ankle chains had been removed to allow him to traverse the rough ground, and his handcuffs taken off to allow him to retrieve the personal belongings of his victim from nearby bushes. This allowed the prisoner to make a desperate attempt to escape: he knocked one officer to the ground with a tree branch and fled. The police later stated that they shouted warnings as they pursued him, but he failed to stop. They shot him in the head. He died in hospital sometime around 5 pm the same day.

The news media were unanimous in their condemnation of the police's handling of the event, but divided over the eventual outcome. Some thought justice had been done, albeit in a rudimentary fashion. Others spoke of conspiracy and cover-up, suggesting that the man gunned down may not have been the serial killer who had terrorized three districts of the country for the past year. On 13 February 1995, those fears proved to be well-founded. The body of 22-year-old Nelsiwe Langa was found, strangled with her own underwear, the grim signature of both 'The Cleveland Strangler' and 'The Atteridgeville Strangler'. If David Selepe, the man police had shot, really had killed the women in Cleveland, then a copycat killer was now on the loose. Or, perhaps even more chillingly, the real Atteridgeville Strangler had been out there the whole time.

A new beginning in South Africa

The 'rainbow nation' of post-apartheid South Africa was formed after the first fully democratic elections in 1994. Nelson Mandela, the previously jailed President of the African National Congress, was elected president of the country: a nation riven by racial violence looked towards the future with hope and optimism. Those who were poor, young and black were the ones with the brightest dreams, suddenly offered the promise of a future of freedom, peace and prosperity. It was exactly this demographic that would be preyed upon by The Atteridgeville Strangler. He would exploit their youthful enthusiasm and desire to better themselves in order to lure them to their deaths. By the time he was caught as many as 40 victims would lie rotting under the fierce African sun in the veldts outside Pretoria and Johannesburg.

In 1993, just as the new South Africa was starting to emerge, Moses Sithole was stepping out from the notorious Pretoria Central Prison. For the first time in four years, he was a free man.

Sithole had been picked out at an identity parade in 1989 by a woman who claimed she had been raped. He was sentenced to seven years for the crime, though he always protested his innocence. He would later claim that it was this injustice that led him to wreak revenge on South African society, and even went so far as to claim that he selected his victims because they resembled the woman who had made the allegation against him. Upon release, he founded a charity called 'Youth Against Human Abuse' an organization ostensibly dedicated to reuniting orphaned children with their families. It was exactly the sort of organization that would flourish in the spirit of 'truth and reconciliation' that was prevalent at the time. Sithole himself could have been a poster-boy for the vibrant new nation: handsome, intelligent and impeccably dressed, he was attractive and charismatic, and even whilst still behind bars in Pretoria prison he was attracting the attention of young women. He met his future wife through a fellow prisoner; soon she was a regular visitor. As soon as he was released on parole, he moved in with her in Soshanguve, Pretoria. They would marry three months after the birth of their daughter, Bridgette.

To the outside world, then, Sithole was a fine, upstanding citizen. The 'Youth Against Human Abuse' organization

Moses Sithole, the 'ABC' Killer.

held meetings in a local school, discussing how to prevent abuse against children and women. On business cards and other official forms, Sithole gave his sister's phone number in Wattville, Atteridgeville as the contact number. Anyone who rang was greeted by the voice of a well-spoken female, who dutifully passed on messages to Moses. They were left with the impression that they had spoken to his secretary, further enhancing the killer's claim that he ran a legitimate and trustworthy organization. Nobody but Sithole himself knew that he harboured a murderous grudge against young black women, and that beneath the respectable exterior lurked a cold-blooded killer.

On 16 July 1994, South Africa's Brixton Murder and Robbery Unit first came to realize that a dangerous predator was at work in their area. The body of an 18-year-old schoolgirl was found with messages written on her inner thighs. In black ink her killer had scrawled: 'She a beach and I am not fighting with you please'. Then, on the other thigh: 'We must stay here for as long as you don't understand'. They interpreted 'She a beach' to mean 'She was a bitch', and the last line to be an ominous warning that there would be further victims if the killer was not caught. They would turn out to be right on both counts.

The Cleveland murders

Cleveland is an industrial suburb to the east of Johannesburg, the largest and most prosperous city in South Africa. It lies on the main M2 freeway and close to the train stations of neighbouring Heriotdale and Geldenhuis. In between the residential areas, Johannesburg's urban sprawl is here increasingly punctuated with wastelands and fields that are only rarely visited. It was in these areas that the first bodies were found. By September, eight had been discovered: all women, all young, all smartly dressed and all black. Three had been found in the same location, as if the killer were 'reclaiming' that spot anew each time a body was removed. In October, a further body was discovered near Geldenhuis train station. The police immediately noticed that this, too, was the body of a young black female. Even more apparent was the manner of her death, which connected her with the Cleveland victims. Each woman was found strangled by an item of her own clothing. Most had had their clothes pulled up or down to expose their breasts and genitals, and had underwear stuffed into their mouths or placed over their faces. It seemed highly likely that a single perpetrator was responsible for all 11 murders.

The Brixton police called in Micki Pistorius, South Africa's first ever psychological profiler, to help. She had just finished working on an investigation into another serial killer, the so-called 'Station Strangler', Norman Afzal Simons. He had been arrested in early 1994 and had later been convicted of the murder of 22 boys in the Western Cape area. In the Cleveland case, Pistorius concluded that the suspect for whom the police were looking was a black male in his mid-twenties to early thirties, and that he was probably attractive and had access to an expensive car. She also told them that he was intelligent and likely to be following media reports on the investigation. In the light of this, the police made a direct appeal to the killer at a press conference in mid-October, asking him to hand himself in. They also requested help from the public in identifying the victims and providing information on any possible suspects. A reward of R200,000 (around £20,000 or $32,000) was also offered in return.

Partly as a result of the press conference, many of the Cleveland victims were identified. They were all young women from respectable homes, and most had jobs or were in full-time education – a teacher, a nurse, a cashier, a student. Many came from Pretoria or the surrounding area, leading the police to look more closely at recent murders in and around that city, about 80 kilometres (50 miles) from Johannesburg. Two women had been found by a cattle-watcher in a field, both neatly dressed and strangled with their own clothing. By talking to friends and families of the victims, the police began to build a picture of their last known movements. In November, the body of 24-year-old Refilwe Amanda Mokale was discovered by the M2 freeway in Heriotdale. Her tragic death would give the police their first real breakthrough in the case.

On the day before she disappeared, Refilwe, a fashion design student, had made an appointment to meet a man about a job opportunity. She had spoken to him in Pretoria, where she went to college, and witnesses were able to describe what he looked like. Several had been approached by the man with the same job offer, so police were confident the identikit they later released to the media was accurate. He was a black male aged 25–30 years old, who spoke Zulu. He had openly approached numerous women in the Pretoria area, so was evidently not overly concerned about being seen. The police now knew what he looked like: the hunt was on for his name.

Several more bodies were identified, and the employer of one of them, 32-year-old Joyce Thakane Mashabela, received a curious phone call five days after she went missing. A man identifying himself as 'Moses Sima' claimed to have found her identity papers whilst out walking through a nearby veldt. The employer passed on the name and address of the caller to Joyce's family, who visited him in order to retrieve the documents. The man was adamant he had nothing to do with her disappearance, and the matter was not pursued.

It was at this point that police arrested David Abraham Selepe, the man they would later shoot and kill. He appeared to be a strong suspect – not only did he match the psychological profile, but he also lived in the area and had a job teaching female students. In addition, a woman had contacted the police to say that David Selepe had offered her a job, but then attempted to rape her. Selepe had recently fled to the neighbouring country of Mozambique, where the police managed to corner him and arrest him. In the boot of his Mercedes Benz they found newspaper cuttings relating to the Cleveland murders and shoe prints that suggested that someone might have been locked inside the car in the recent past. What must at the time have seemed like a great policing success soon turned into a public relations disaster, however. Selepe's death at the hands of the police led to numerous conspiracy theories, and to this day it is unclear just how involved he was with the Cleveland murders. Although he confessed to 15 killings, he could not lead the police to any remains they did not already know about. He claimed to have two accomplices working with him – one called Tito and one called Mandla.

The only man of the latter name who could be traced was already in prison, so had a perfect alibi. The man named Tito volunteered DNA samples that failed to match any found at the crime scenes. Any lingering hope the police had of an early resolution to the case evaporated with the discovery of a new body on a patch of veldt near Village Deep, around 10 kilometres (6 miles) outside of Cleveland. Nelsiwe Langa, 22, had been strangled with her own underwear and left with her smart clothes pushed up above her waist. The hallmarks of the Cleveland and Pretoria killer were obvious to the investigation team. Their killer had struck again. And very soon afterwards, word reached them from the township of Arreridgeville, west of Pretoria. Bodies had begun to be found there, too – and the modus operandi of the killer was once again similar.

The Atteridgeville murders

Eight new corpses were found in the six months after the death of the chief suspect in the case, David Selepe. All but one were young black females, and all were found in the Atteridgeville area. The exception was two-year-old Sibusiso Ndlangamandla, whose body was found in close proximity to that of his mother, Letta. The young mother had disappeared earlier in April after going to meet a man in Pretoria about a job offer. Having no one to look after her son, she took him with her. The pathologist could not determine how Sibusiso died, or whether his death came before or after the death of his mother. He had a bloody bruise on his head, but might have died of exposure. It could not be ruled out that he had seen his mother being killed and died wandering, cold and frightened, through the field where her body lay.

A ninth victim was discovered in nearby Rosslyn. Police

were puzzled by the fact that some of the victims had not been bound, yet others had their hands tied in front of them, and others still had their hands tied behind their backs. As the police struggled to work out which cases were related, the grim regularity of fresh discoveries of bodies continued into the summer. Despite the massive media coverage, and the widespread publication of the identikit picture, police were no closer to catching the killer. They turned to the famous retired FBI criminal profiler Robert Ressler for help. He was a veteran of dozens of such cases, and was first to coin the English term 'serial killer'. In 1985, he founded the FBI's Violent Criminal Apprehension Program, a nationwide database for tracking serial killers.

From his base at the Holiday Inn in Pretoria, Ressler's first job was to try to untangle the mystery of David Selepe and the 'second killer' who remained on the loose. His conclusion was that Selepe was responsible for some of the Cleveland killings, but worked with an accomplice who remained at large and was now killing women in the Atteridgeville area. Ressler later spoke at a press conference at which he outlined his thoughts about the killer. He was avidly watched by Moses Sithole, who later remarked that he thought Ressler 'talked shit'.

Inspector Vivian Bieldt also called on the expertise of Scotland Yard in London, the FBI and Interpol, as well as consulting entomologist Dr Mervyn Mansell of the Agricultural Research Council in Pretoria. Bieldt wondered if the maggots feeding on the corpses could help identify the precise time of death, and Mansell confirmed that in certain cases they could. On 17 September 1995, Mansell was asked to put that theory into practice when police found another body in a field at the Van Dyk Mine near Boksburg, just over an hour's drive south of Pretoria. As he packed his bag to leave, he received a second call from Inspector Bieldt. It was not one body, he was told, but five. By the time Dr Mansell arrived at the scene that number had doubled again. It was the most horrific discovery thus far: a mass grave of young women in various stages of decomposition, some of them left just feet apart.

The Boksburg murders

Some of the bodies were severely decomposed, with clusters of maggots the size of melons swarming through their flesh. Others were relatively untouched, showing they had been left fairly recently. On the jeans of one victim were stains that showed she had wet herself in terror. It is probable that the killer led her on a horrific tour through the field of corpses before delivering her to the same fate as the others.

The revelation of the discoveries at Boksburg led to a renewed media frenzy, during which even President Nelson Mandela visited the crime scene to appeal for the public's help. There was speculation that the murders might be linked to 'black magic' and human sacrifice, because various candles, mirrors, feathers and knives were found close by. A man called Absalom Sangweni, who lived in a caravan in Boksburg, came forward to say he had seen a man lead a woman into the field and had even warned him that the path led nowhere, but admitted that he hadn't got a good look at the man's face.

By accurately dating the times of death of the victims, a pattern began to emerge of the killer's behaviour. Placed in order of death rather than in order of discovery, it became clear that the serial killer had refined his method over time, moving from first not tying up his victims to tying them with their hands in front of them, and then more recently tying them with their hands behind their backs. The first victims were throttled; later the murderer progressed to strangling them, using increasingly sophisticated methods to control precisely how long they took to die. The last of his victims were fiendishly tied so that they would eventually strangle themselves as they struggled to be free. Sithole was by now horribly expert in the practice and his murders had evolved to a new level of sadistic evil. He had become contemptuous and arrogant – no longer bothering even to conceal the bodies of his victims, and dumping ten of them within the same 300 metre (328 yard) radius.

This confidence was misplaced, however, and ultimately led to the killer's capture. A handbag found at the Boksburg crime scene was traced to one of the victims, Amelia Rapodile. Her family told the police that she had arranged to meet a man about a job offer on the day she disappeared. They also remembered the man's name: he was called Moses Sithole.

The manhunt

Sithole was not at his home address. He and his wife had separated on 31 July 1995, after a heated argument over school keys. The school where Sithole held his 'Youth Against Human Abuse' organization had requested the keys, but for reasons unknown Sithole had taken them and held on to them. Perhaps there was something at the school that Sithole didn't want anyone to find: at any rate, he became enraged when his wife criticized him, packed his bags and left. Sithole's sister Kwazi hadn't seen him for weeks, either. But the police would soon be on Sithole's tail: he was by now spiralling rapidly out of control and was in no mood to keep a low profile. Just a week after the media frenzy at Boksburg, Sithole killed 20-year-old Agnes Sibongile Mbuli and dumped her body at Kleinfontein train station a few miles east of Boksburg. On the day that her body was found, Sithole decided it was time to make direct contact with the press.

Tamsen de Beer, a reporter at *The Star* newspaper, was the one who took the call. A man who called himself Joseph Magwena stated that: 'I am the man that is so highly wanted'. He claimed he planned to surrender, and gave details about the crimes that only the killer could know. De Beer notified the police, who arranged to record the calls and encouraged the reporter to try to arrange a meeting with the caller. Though the meeting was set up, the police failed to catch Sithole, in part due to officers blundering into the meeting zone without realizing an undercover operation was under way. The investigators decided to go public with Sithole's name and photograph, which was soon emblazoned on the front page of every newspaper in the country. With the heat on him, Sithole contacted his brother-in-law to ask for help. In particular, he wanted a gun in order to defend himself from the pursuing police. His brother-in-law Maxwell agreed to meet Sithole at the Mintex Factory in nearby Benoni where he worked, in order to hand over the requested firearm. Then he telephoned the police.

Sithole almost escaped the trap laid for him a second time. Inspector Francis Mulovhedzi was posing as a security guard when Sithole approached the Mintex Factory gates and asked to see Maxwell. Two other guards, who were unaware that Mulovhedzi was not the 'new guy' in the job, ordered him to go and fetch the worker, but Mulovhedzi refused because he didn't want to let Sithole out of his sight. What happened next is open to dispute: according to Mulovhedzi, Sithole was spooked and suddenly ran. When Mulovhedzi caught up with him, Sithole came at him with an axe and so the police officer shot him in the stomach and the leg. Sithole maintained in court that he was shot without warning at the factory gates. Whatever the real truth, the police finally had their man. He was taken to the Glynwood Hospital in Benoni, operated on and placed in police custody once he had recovered.

The trial

On 21 October 1996, a crowded Pretoria Supreme Court watched with horrified incredulity as the video of Sithole's confession was played. Relaxed, suave, dressed in a red leather hat, he munched an apple whilst he spoke in a casual manner about murdering innocent young women. The conversation was recorded by three fellow inmates who hoped to profit from providing such valuable evidence.

In an hour-long, self-righteous soliloquy, dragging on a cigarette, Sithole explained how he lured the women to remote spots and killed them in revenge for the injustice he perceived had been done to him by society. He showed absolutely no remorse. The prosecution called witness after witness to testify that Sithole had in fact committed rapes for which he was never charged. They then moved on to the harrowing details of the murders themselves. Sithole was charged with killing 37 women and the two-year-old toddler Sibusiso Ndlangamandla.

In addition, he faced 40 counts of rape and six of robbery. He pleaded not guilty to all charges. He stared calmly at the dozens of young women who testified that Sithole had offered jobs to their friends and family-members shortly before they disappeared. With so many crimes to prosecute, the trial dragged on for over a year.

Inevitably, finally, Sithole was found guilty on all charges. The judge was the notoriously hardline Mr Justice David Curlewis, who lamented that he could not pronounce a death sentence on Sithole; the rainbow nation had declared such sentences unconstitutional the previous year. Instead, Sithole was given a record 2,410 years in prison. He would, the judge added dryly, be eligible for parole in 930 years.

It was later revealed that Sithole was HIV positive, and at the time of his arrest it was estimated that he would only survive for another eight years. As a prisoner in the new South Africa, however, he is entitled to free medical care, and his health to date has remained good. He was moved from the maximum security C-Max wing of Pretoria Central Prison to Sun City Prison south of Johannesburg, and from there to a private facility in Mangaung, Free State in 2012. Sithole appealed against that move on the grounds that it would 'inconvenience' him and disrupt his university studies. Judge Mathilda Masipa remarked, 'Your application as it stands has no merit and is dismissed'. In the Sesotho language his current place of incarceration, Mangaung, means 'place of cheetahs'. It was taken over by the Department of Correctional Services in 2013 after the private contractors,

G4S, were found to have used uncertified staff. Prisoners alleged they were subjected to forced injections of anti-psychotic drugs and electric shock therapy by teams of wardens nicknamed 'Ninjas'. South Africa's *Mail & Guardian* paper summed the prison up as 'a private hell'.

Sithole has more than 900 years left to serve there.

CHAPTER NINE

The Zodiac Killer

On a frosty December night in 1968 in Vallejo, California, Stella Borges was driving her mother-in-law and daughter along Lake Herman Road. When her car approached the Benicia water pumping station, the headlights picked out a station wagon parked in a nearby exit. As Borges got closer she realized, with mounting horror, that two bodies lay sprawled beside the car. She accelerated to 110 kilometres per hour (68 miles per hour) and raced towards the nearby city of Benicia to get help. Flashing her headlights and honking her horn she flagged down a police car. Just minutes later the police were on the scene.

Seventeen-year-old David Faraday was still breathing, but unresponsive; he had a bullet wound in the head. His date for that night, 16-year-old Betty Lou Jensen, evidently ran for her life away from the gunman. She made it 9 metres (10 yards). Shot five times in the back, she was already dead.

'I never saw so much blood on the side of the road in my life,' an ambulance attendant told reporters at the time.

1647710

This is the Zodiac speaking.
I am the murderer of the
taxi driver over by
Washington St & Maple St last
night, to prove this here is
a blood stoined piece of his
shirt. I am the same man
who did in the people in the
nouth bay a-ea.
The S.F. Police could have caught
me last night if they had

A chilling letter from the Zodiac Killer.

Thus begins the most mysterious unsolved serial killer case in modern history. Although the world didn't know it yet, the two teenagers lying on the roadside in fresh pools of blood would later be identified as the first victims of the infamous 'Zodiac Killer'.

The Zodiac's genesis

One of the most extraordinary decades in US history was drawing to a close. The 1960s was a period of unparalleled social change and domestic division in the United States. The year that ended with the Zodiac's first murders saw the Army occupy three American cities and the National Guard patrol a dozen more in the wake of riots sparked by the assassination of Martin Luther King. Democrat candidate for the White House Robert Kennedy was gunned down two months later. Incumbent President Lyndon Johnson had already announced he would not stand for re-election, all too aware of how divisive his policy to widen the war in Vietnam had become. The liberal 'New Deal Coalition' that had brought the country through the challenges of the Great Depression, the Second World War and the Cuban Missile Crisis was unravelling.

Republican Richard Nixon was elected to the White House in November 1968. He promised to restore order and security to a country that had begun to feel as though it had lost its way. Nowhere was the division in US society more starkly seen than in the West Coast San Francisco Bay area. It was here that hippies proclaimed 1967 to be the 'Summer of Love'. Conservative America's bemusement with the 'flower children' had rapidly turned to mistrust and fear. Republican Governor of California Ronald Reagan had already begun to crack down on the drug-taking, lovemaking and peacenik protests. In Death Valley, cult leader Charles Manson preached to his 'Family' about a coming civil war and the end of the world.

The very day after David Faraday and Betty Lou Jensen were murdered, *Apollo* 8 blasted off from the Kennedy Space Center on a mission to orbit the Moon. They took the famous 'Earthrise' photo of planet Earth viewed from space, and broadcast the creation story from the Book of Genesis to an enthralled nation. The astronauts signed off with the words 'good night, good luck, a Merry Christmas and God bless all of you – all of you on the good Earth'. Commander Frank Borman later received a telegram from a stranger that summed up the mood in the United States. It read 'Thank you *Apollo* 8. You saved 1968'.

On 21 July 1969, Neil Armstrong would take his famous 'one small step' on to the surface of the Moon. By then, back on Earth, the Zodiac killer had murdered again.

Independence

The man who called Vallejo Police Headquarters in the early hours of 5 July 1969 spoke methodically and without emotion, as if reading from a script. He wanted to inform the authorities of a double murder, roughly 1.5 kilometres (¾ miles) east on Columbus Parkway, in a public park. When asked for his identity and location, he declared that he was the killer not only of the two victims shot half an hour earlier, but also of Betty Lou and David in 1968. This was the first indication that the Vallejo police were dealing not with two unrelated crimes, but with a serial killer.

By the time of the call, police were already on the scene at Blue Rocks Spring, alerted by three teenagers who had come across the couple. Nineteen-year-old Mike Mageau was found slumped against the right rear tyre of a brown Corvair, bleeding heavily from gunshot wounds to the neck, leg and arm. Darlene Ferrin, 22, was in the driver's seat, suffering from multiple gunshot wounds, and barely alive. She was pronounced Dead On Arrival at the nearby Kaiser Foundation Hospital. The anonymous caller was wrong about the 'double murder', however: Mageau, despite his horrific injuries, survived.

The story Mageau told the police was the first glimpse into the character of the Zodiac killer. Mageau stated that a white male had approached the car shining a bright flashlight and, without saying a word, began firing 'again and again'. When he finally finished his murderous volley, he turned and walked back towards his own car. Mageau cried out in pain, and the assailant returned to fire two more shots into him, and two more into Darlene. He then walked back to his car and sped off at high speed. Mageau failed to get a good look at either the suspect or his car, but believed the man was 'beefy' with a large face and driving a light brown vehicle.

Whoever attacked Darlene and Mike took a huge risk: it was the night of 4 July, Independence Day in the United States, and thus a national holiday. Many people were out and about that night, heading to and from firework displays and parties. Any offender brazen enough to attack in such circumstances, and to even brag about it shortly afterwards, was likely to strike again. And so it proved.

Donald Harden hard at work
decoding the Zodiac Killer's message.

'The most dangerous anamal'

In August 1969, three separate newspapers received almost identical letters claiming to be from the man who had attacked the four youngsters at Lake Herman Road and Blue Rocks Spring. The letters included information about the crime scenes that only the killer or the police could possibly know. The *Vallejo Times Herald*, *San Francisco Chronicle* and *San Francisco Examiner* also each received one-third of a 408-symbol cryptogram that the killer claimed would reveal his identity. The papers all published their part of the cryptogram, along with the killer's ominous threats to kill again.

Within a week the cryptogram was broken by a husband-and-wife team of local teachers, Bettye and Donald Harden. The message deciphered was as follows (complete with spelling and grammatical errors): 'I like killing people because it is so much fun it is more fun than killing wild game in the forrest because man is the most dangerous anamal of all to kill something gives me the most thrilling experience it is even better than getting your rocks off with a girl the best part of it is that when I die I will be reborn in paradice and thei have killed will become my slaves I will not give you my name because you will try to slow down or stop my collecting of slaves for my afterlife'.

A further 18 characters appeared to be gibberish, there only to pad out the code – if the killer meant anything by these letters then they have not, as yet, been deciphered. Although the included message had claimed that breaking the cipher would reveal the killer's identity, the actual text gave the police precious little to go on in terms of solving the case. Indeed, the author suggested that he wanted to continue his 'collecting of slaves', which hinted that he intended to kill again. Tip-offs poured in to the police, and dozens of suspects were questioned, but the killer remained at large.

Bloodshed at Berryessa

Summer had faded into autumn when students Cecelia Shepherd and Bryan Hartnell took a trip out to the idyllic shores of Lake Berryessa, around 80 kilometres (50 miles) north of Vallejo. It was Cecelia who first noticed that a man seemed to be watching them on that September evening. Bryan, without his glasses on, only became aware of a problem when the man was practically upon them, holding a gun. He was wearing a bizarre costume: a square hood with clip-on sunglasses covered his head, and a bib came down over his chest. On it was sewn the same 'crosshair' symbol that the Zodiac signed his letters with.

The man told the two youngsters that he just escaped from prison and needed money and a car in order to get to Mexico. Hartnell offered his wallet and car keys, and tried to keep the assailant calm. But the man ordered Cecelia to tie Bryan up and, once she had done so, he tightened the binds and tied her up, too. As they lay helpless on the ground, he took out a knife that police would later estimate to be 25–30 centimetres (10–12 inches) long. He used it to stab Bryan six times in the back, then Cecelia a total of ten times as she writhed and spun in desperate terror. He then calmly walked away, taking neither the car keys nor the wallet.

Bryan and Cecelia managed to free themselves and, eventually, summon help from a fisherman out on the lake.

WANTED

SAN FRANCISCO POLICE DEPARTMENT

NO. 90-69   <u>WANTED FOR MURDER</u>   OCTOBER 18, 1969

ORIGINAL DRAWING   AMENDED DRAWING

Supplementing our Bulletin 87-69 of October 13, 1969. Additional information has developed the above amended drawing of murder suspect known as "ZODIAC".

WMA, 35-45 Years, approximately 5'8", Heavy Build, Short Brown Hair, possibly with Red Tint, Wears Glasses. Armed with 9 MM Automatic.

Available for comparison: Slugs, Casings, Latents, Handwriting.

<u>ANY INFORMATION:</u>
Inspectors Armstrong & Toschi
Homicide Detail   THOMAS J. CAHILL
CASE NO. 696314   CHIEF OF POLICE

The Zodiac Killer from 1969

But by the time an ambulance had made it out to the remote spot each of the victims had been bleeding heavily for more than an hour. Cecelia died in hospital two days later. She was 22 years old. Bryan, incredibly, survived. The police who questioned him at his bedside already knew who was responsible for the attack: it was the latest atrocity by the Zodiac killer.

This time, the Zodiac not only rang the police to take credit (from a pay phone traced to downtown Napa); he also left a taunting message written with a marker pen on the door of Bryan Hartnell's white Kharmann Ghia car. It gave the dates of the previous attacks, along with the date and time of this one: 'Sept 27 – 69 – 6:30'. The Zodiac added 'by knife' to signal the change in his weapon of choice.

Though he couldn't describe the face of his attacker, Bryan could at least furnish the investigating officers with some fresh details about the elusive Zodiac. The man was wearing pleated, old style trousers, black or dark blue and a dark blue 'windbreaker' style jacket. He was heavy-set, and 1.7–1.8 metres (5.5–5.9 feet) tall. He spoke in a drawl that Bryan described as 'distinctive', but he couldn't place the accent. Bryan glimpsed greasy dark brown hair through the eyeholes of the man's mask.

The police also discovered footprints that were made by a distinctive 'Wing Walker' boot, size 10 ½. They lifted a palm-print from the telephone the man had used in Napa, but the technician smudged it during the lifting process, ruining its evidential value. The Zodiac had struck in daylight, in staggeringly theatrical fashion, and he had – just, only just – got away with it. His next attack would bring terror to the very heart of West Coast 1960s America: San Francisco.

Presidio Heights attack

On Saturday 11 October 1969, San Francisco cab driver Paul Stine picked up a fare at the corner of Mason and Geary Streets in Union Square, San Francisco. His passenger asked to be taken to an area near the Presidio at the northern tip of the peninsula. It is not known whether the man who climbed into his cab sat in the rear or the front seat with Stine. What is known is that the man he picked up was the Zodiac killer.

It was just before 10 pm when Stine arrived at the destination that he'd entered in his log, the corner of Washington and Maple Street. For reasons unknown, he then proceeded one block further west, to the junction of Washington and Cherry Street. Nobody reported hearing the gunshot that then blew apart Stine's head. Three teenagers noticed the cab parked opposite their house, and watched a man in the front seat rifle through the dead driver's pockets, taking his wallet, ID and the keys to his cab. The body of Paul Stine was slumped in the murderer's lap, meaning that the killer must have been covered in blood as he calmly walked away north, towards the park.

The witnesses described a white man in his early forties, around 1.7 metres (5 feet 6 inches) tall, of heavy build, wearing dark brown trousers and a navy blue or black 'Parka' jacket. He had reddish-blond hair cut in a 'crew-cut' style and was wearing glasses. But instead of that description, the police officers who raced to the scene were told to be on the look out for a black male. When a patrol car passed a white man in glasses casually strolling towards the park minutes later, it didn't stop. Only when the description was corrected did it screech to a halt and speed back in pursuit.

But by then it was too late: despite the use of police dogs and search lights, the suspect had melted into the night.

It was an agonizingly close near-miss. The Zodiac would give a detailed, mocking account of it in a series of letters to the *San Francisco Chronicle*, claiming that the police even stopped and talked to him at one point. In the first of his letters, sent two days after the murder, he enclosed a bloodied piece of Paul Stine's shirt to ensure that the journalists and police knew that he was a killer rather than a crank or hoaxer. The police thus had to take seriously his next ominous threat: 'School children make nice targets'.

The death machine

The Zodiac's 13 October letter to the *San Francisco Chronicle* was read aloud to the nation's news media by San Francisco Police Department Captain Martin Lee: 'I think I shall wipe out a school bus some morning, just shoot out the front tyre and then pick off the kiddies as they come bouncing out'.

The threat caused panic across California, and particularly in San Francisco. Buses changed routes daily, marked and unmarked police cars followed ahead or behind them, and fixed-wing aircraft patrolled overhead. The Police instructed school bus drivers to keep their buses moving 'at all costs' and advised passengers to lie on the floor in the event of an attack. The authorities were deluged with calls from members of the public across the United States offering tips and outlining suspicions and fears.

After a couple of weeks, the danger appeared to have subsided. But then the Zodiac wrote another letter, on 10 November. He began by claiming to have now killed seven people – two more than the police had thus far associated with him. Then, enclosing detailed diagrams to back up his claim, he outlined his plan to carry out a terrorist attack on schoolchildren by using a bomb he described as 'the death machine'. He also sent another cryptogram, containing 340 mysterious characters. To this day the Zodiac's message has never been decoded. There have been countless attempts and claims to have broken the code, but none has been widely accepted as successful.

On 20 December 1969, exactly one year after the murders of David Faraday and Betty Lou Jensen, the Zodiac posted a further letter to the prominent lawyer Melvin Belli, along with another swatch of Paul Stine's bloody shirt. He claimed to have now killed eight, and stated that the 'death machine' was taking longer to prepare than he had imagined. He wished Belli a 'happy Christmass [sic]' and asked him for help in controlling 'this thing in me'.

There were several further communications which purported to be from the Zodiac, though most are now considered to be fakes. A greetings card sent to the *Chronicle* urged people to wear 'Zodiac' buttons (badges), and a map of the Mount Diablo area was sent with another cipher that claimed to reveal where a bomb had been planted. This communication claimed that the Zodiac's body count had by now risen to 12. Again, the cipher has never been broken. On 27 October 1970, *Chronicle* reporter Paul Avery received a Halloween card that seemed to threaten his life and also appeared to claim that the Zodiac's running total of victims had reached 14. Despite the claims, however, no further murders were definitively linked to the killer.

The Zodiac's legacy

Why did the slaughter suddenly stop? It is yet another mystery in this most mysterious of cases. Some have suggested that the Zodiac killer was arrested and jailed for some unrelated crime, and this ended his career. Others posit that he died, or moved away from the San Francisco area to assume another identity elsewhere. Perhaps, others argue, he simply grew bored and ended his reign of terror because it no longer amused or thrilled him. There's one more theory, perhaps the most troubling of all – that the later Zodiac letters are true, and that the body count provided in them is accurate. In one letter the author wrote 'when I commit my murders they shall look like routine robberies, killings of anger and a few fake accidents etc'. Could the Zodiac really have killed, as he went on to claim, a total of 37 people without the police even realizing the deaths were murders?

The first serial killer to attain legendary status was Jack the Ripper, and like Jack 'The Zodiac Killer' he evaded capture. Perhaps this explains why these two killers remain so fascinating to researchers today. Between them, they helped to define what we think of as the 'classic serial killer': an evil genius who taunts the authorities and remains forever one step ahead of them. Countless films and books have been inspired by the Zodiac's trademark method of sending cryptic messages that only the brightest minds could crack. Although in truth such individuals are incredibly rare, they have given birth to an entire mythology, one that remains 'box office' to this day.

Few crimes remain vivid in the collective memory of the United States of America, the home of the serial killer.

An estimated 85 per cent of all the world's serial killers operate in the States, for reasons that remain hotly debated by experts. Even those with far higher body counts than the Zodiac's five are soon forgotten, and yet he remains the killer that most intrigues, fascinates and horrifies all those who read about him.

Unlike in the case of Jack the Ripper, there remains the possibility that The Zodiac Killer is still alive, still out there somewhere; that he could still, even now, kill again – or be caught. In 2005, William Speer was convicted of murdering 14-year-old Linda Harmon after DNA taken at the scene of the crime was finally matched to him. Speer had remained free since committing the crime 37 years earlier, in 1968.

But in 2004, the San Francisco Police Department officially closed the Zodiac Killer case (although it has remained open with The California Justice Department). It was the first time in their history that they had closed an unsolved homicide case. 'The police shall never catch me, because I have been too clever for them,' the Zodiac wrote in a letter to the *San Francisco Chronicle*. While the case has since been re-opened by the San Francisco Police Department, tragically, it appears as though the killer's prediction has been right.

CHAPTER TEN

Charles Sobhraj, 'The Serpent'

Unlike most young Westerners arriving in Thailand in December 1975, Stephanie Parry wasn't looking for adventure, a good time or spiritual enlightenment: she was just looking for her associate, Vitali 'Ved' Hakim. Like thousands of others in the 1960s and 1970s, Ved had gone east along the 'Hippie Trail' that led from his birthplace in Turkey through Iran to India, Nepal and Thailand. He'd sampled the black cakes of pure hashish and the 'Thai sticks' of premium marijuana buds skewered on stems. Soon he started importing them to the Mediterranean paradise of Ibiza, selling to the local sunseekers to pay for his drop-out lifestyle. He moved into heroin, to make more money, then started taking it himself, which ate into his bottom line. Before he knew it he was out of his depth. Stephanie was due to pick up a false-bottomed suitcase full of drugs and take it back to Spain, where she lived. But Ved had suddenly stopped returning her calls.

The 24-year-old Frenchwoman had already trawled the $4-a-night hotels of the area in her hunt for Ved, with no success. On 9 December, she rang a phone number she'd been given, and asked to speak with Alain Gautier. She'd been told that Ved was last seen in his company.

Alain did, indeed, know Ved Hakim. He had been introduced to the long-haired dealer a few weeks earlier by another tourist who hung out in the lobby of the nearby Atlantic Hotel. Alain had offered to take Ved to the mines at Chanthaburi, on the border with Cambodia, in order to buy rubies, sapphires and other fine gemstones at whole-sale prices. But Ved ended up in the grounds of the Siam Country Club in Chonburi, just outside the beach resort of Pattaya. He had been drugged, then beaten viciously with wooden boards. As he lay bruised and bleeding on the ground, he was covered in gasoline and burnt alive. His charred remains were discovered on 28 November by a rice-farmer working in the fields nearby.

Alain Gautier's real name was Hotchand Bhaonani Gurumukh Sobhraj, though he rarely used it, assuming instead the identities of countless tourists whose passports he stole. The American press later called him 'The Charles Manson of the East'; the police nicknamed him 'The Serpent' because of his exceptional talent for deception; he himself took the name 'Charles Sobhraj' whilst at boarding school in Paris where he was famous for the impersonation he used to do of Charlie Chaplin. Sobhraj, in his various guises, was top of Interpol's most-wanted list and sought by authorities in Thailand, Pakistan, Afghanistan, France, Greece, Turkey, Iran, Nepal and Hong Kong. The charge list included robbery, drug-offences, prison escapes and murder.

Alain agreed to meet Stephanie Parry in the foyer of the President Hotel, where she was staying. He told her he had an urgent message for her from Ved.

The Thailand murders

Stephanie Parry's body was found washed up on a Pattaya beach on 14 December. Thai police did not yet suspect a serial killer might be in their midst. They just knew a murder had been committed: this woman had not drowned but had been strangled with such force that her neck bones had broken. They made no connection to the earlier death of Teresa Knowlton, whose bikini-clad body had been found by a fisherman on 18 October floating in the water off Pattaya beach. The young American woman had been drinking and taking drugs, so investigators assumed that she had drowned accidentally. Still unidentified, she was photographed and then buried at the local Sawang Boribbon Cemetery. The similarly unidentified body of Ved Hakim was later buried close by. Three deaths, two of them murders; a tragic period for the Thai police, but nothing that would raise undue concern in the popular resort of Pattaya.

On 12 December two Dutch tourists arrived at Bangkok airport and were greeted by the beaming smile of Charles Sobhraj, whom they knew as the gem-dealer Alain Dupuis. He insisted they got a cab back to his place rather than stay in one of Bangkok's seedy hotels.

Apartment number 504 was on the top floor of Kanit House, just off Sukhumvit, the longest road in Thailand and the main thoroughfare of the capital, Bangkok. The many adjoining *sois* (sub-streets) of Sukhumvit bustle with cafes, bars and the red-light districts of Nana Plaza and Soi Cowboy. The home of 'Alain Gautier' was always full of young people hanging out, getting high and then getting mysteriously ill. Dysentery was a common problem for travellers to Thailand,

Charles Sobhraj and his girlfriend Marie-Andrée Leclerc.

and those who showed the symptoms of it at Kanit House were grateful to Alain for nursing them back to health. He ended up with a small 'family' of such people who felt they owed him a debt of gratitude. There were three French travellers, Dominique, Yannick and François, and a young Indian by the name of Ajay Chowdhury, who would do anything for Alain. Then there was the French-Canadian medical secretary Marie-Andrée Leclerc, who had left her fiancé in July to become Alain's live-in girlfriend, changing her name to 'Monique' at his insistence.

The newcomers were Dutch students called Henricus 'Henk' Bitanja and Cornelia 'Cocky' Hemker. They were backpacking their way around the world before they settled down to get married. They'd saved up for five years before setting out from Amsterdam for their trip of a lifetime eight months earlier. Cornelia was wearing a sapphire ring sold to her in Hong Kong at a bargain price by Alain. He had promised to take her to the gem mines, and teach Henk how to grade precious stones. The trip to the mines would have to be postponed, however, because shortly after arriving the young Dutch couple fell ill with the same symptoms that afflicted so many of Alain's houseguests.

Their gracious host had spiked their drinks with laxatives and heavy sedatives, producing stomach cramps, diarrhoea and debilitating fatigue, the classic symptoms of dysentery. Sobhraj's favoured drug of choice was Largactyl, a tranquillizer used to treat schizophrenia, which doctors sometimes describe as 'a chemical straightjacket'. Mogadon and Mandrax were also in his cabinet: mixed with alcohol (as they usually were by Sobhraj) the drugs can cause hallucinations and disorientation. After two days, Henk grew scared and insisted Alain take them to a hospital. Later that night their host and his cohort Ajay bundled the couple into his Toyota and drove towards Don Muang Airport and then out through the rice fields, just past the quiet town of Rangsit. When the car stopped and the doors opened the confused young couple stumbled out into the dark night amidst torrential rain. Henk realized they were in terrible trouble and groggily fought with Sobhraj. But the lithe assassin was an expert in karate and had the hulking Ajay to help him beat Henk to the ground. Together they drowned him in a deep puddle, then turned their attention to Cordelia, smashing in her skull. They doused the pair in gasoline, lit a match and sped away.

The charred bodies were found by village schoolchildren the next day. The Thai police assumed that the young tourists, like Ved before them, were ambushed by one of the bandit-gangs that roamed the roads around Bangkok to steal from wealthy Westerners. They were initially misidentified as two Australian tourists. By the time anyone realized who they really were, or the person they had met just prior to their murders, Charles Sobhraj had cashed the couple's traveller's cheques and flown out of Bangkok to Katmandu. He arrived in Nepal's capital city using the passport of the murdered Henk Bitanja.

The Nepal murders

Connie Jo Bronzich had travelled to Katmandu by bus from Delhi in India. The 28-year-old Californian was trying to escape the violence and mayhem of her home city, Santa Cruz, where her father dealt smack. She was travelling light, but with the emotional baggage of a failed marriage

– and with a serious drug habit. Like most other Westerners, she checked into the Oriental Hotel on Freak Street, the epicentre of the Hippy Trail in Nepal. Soon she met a handsome young Canadian called Laurent Ormond Carrière, who was in the country to climb Mount Everest. The unlikely pair became an item, hanging out in the cafes of Freak Street and taking in the sights. After just a couple of days they were approached by a charming gem-dealer from Bangkok and his beautiful wife.

Connie Jo's horribly mutilated body was found on 22 December near Dhulikel, 30 kilometres (18 miles) south-east of Kathmandu, by the main road through the foothills of the Himalayas to neighbouring Tibet. She was discovered naked, except for a vest that had seared on to her skin after her body had been set alight. She had been repeatedly stabbed in a frenzied attack. Laurent Carrière's whereabouts were unknown at this stage, so he became the chief suspect. In reality his body lay not far from Connie Jo's: his throat had been cut so deeply that his head was almost severed.

As the Nepalese police bagged Connie Jo's body, Charles Sobhraj caught a plane back to Bangkok, where he and Monique planned to spend Christmas. When he arrived back in Thailand, however, he was in for a shock.

Growing suspicion

The 'family' back at Apartment no. 504 read the reports in the *Bangkok Post* daily paper with increasing concern. The press had by now printed pictures of the bodies of the dead tourists, and from them Yannick recognized Cornelia's denim skirt and what the paper described as a 'Made In Holland' T-shirt. Although the police still believed the victims were Australian, Sobhraj's housemates were convinced they were the two Dutch tourists whom 'Alain' and Ajay had supposedly taken to the hospital for treatment. They confided in one of Sobhraj's neighbours, Nadine Gires, who had already raised suspicions about the number of house guests who were falling ill. Together they searched the apartment for evidence, and discovered that many of Henk and Cornelia's possessions had been left behind there. They also found dozens of passports that had been doctored to allow Sobhraj to insert his own photograph into them. Among the passports was one belonging to Stephanie Parry. A piece of hosepipe on top of the refrigerator still smelt of gasoline. With an increasing sense of panic, they realized they had to flee the apartment before Sobhraj returned from Nepal.

None of them much trusted the Thai police, who had a reputation for corruption and incompetence. They considered contacting the French embassy instead, but Alain was known to have many contacts there. In the end, Sobhraj's neighbour Nadine Gires confided in a French businessman she knew and he in turn informed the British embassy. They passed the information on to the Thai police who, as feared, did nothing whatsoever about it.

Dominique, Yannick and François packed their bags and got on the next flight back to Paris. As they left from the departure gate at Bangkok airport, Charles Sobhraj was passing through the arrivals gate on his return from Nepal. It was an incredibly close escape, but he didn't see them. Sobhraj was suspicious, however, because his calls to the apartment had gone unanswered. Rather than risk travelling there himself, he sent his trusted sidekick Ajay to investigate, and it was he that discovered that the trio had fled.

Sobhraj sensed that Thailand was becoming too hot a place in which to operate, and elected to take a plane to safer climes. Incredibly, he chose the country in which he had just committed two murders: Nepal.

Back there, the police had recovered Connie Jo Bronzich's journal. In it she had noted down the name and address of the gem-dealer she had run into: Alain Gautier, 504 Kanit House, Soi Saladaeng, Bangkok. For some reason they did not ask the Thai police to pay the man a visit. And they failed to notice when he paid a visit to them: Sobhraj's numerous stolen passports meant he could travel under assumed identities with complete impunity. He initially left Nepal using Laurent Carrière's passport, which led the Nepalese to conclude that Connie Jo Bronzich had been killed by her new Canadian boyfriend, whom they surmised had then fled the country. The search for his present whereabouts drew a blank, and they puzzled over the identity of the male body in their morgue. Sobhraj idled away his time around Nepal until he felt it was safe to return to Thailand. He figured the Thai police would have lost interest by now; he was right.

But an unlikely new investigator had become interested in him, and this man would ultimately prove to be his nemesis.

Made in Holland

Herman Knippenberg was a young Dutch diplomat working at the embassy in Bangkok. When he was contacted by the relatives of Cornelia and Henk to ask for help in tracing them, he began to investigate their disappearance. He soon heard the rumours about the gem-dealer Alain Gautier, and how visitors to his flat seemed to become ill and vanish shortly afterwards. Cornelia and Henk had written home about meeting with a gem-dealer, and this gave Knippenberg a crucial lead. He contacted the Thai police about the two bodies they had found, one dressed in a 'Made In Holland' T-shirt. They revealed that the two missing Australian tourists initially thought to be the victims had in fact recently turned up alive and well. Knippenberg requested dental records from the Dutch couple's family and positively identified the bodies at last. It turned out to be Cornelia's bra, not her T-shirt, that was 'Made in Holland'. Further investigation revealed the existence of the report the British embassy had sent to Thai police eight weeks earlier. When Knippenberg contacted the British they revealed they also had Henk and Cornelia's travel journal, written in Dutch, which they had not bothered to have translated. When Knippenberg read it he must have felt he was receiving messages from beyond the grave: it ended with them meeting Alain Gautier.

Knippenberg then drew up a report for the Thai police, which outlined the evidence against 'Alain Gautier' of 504 Kanit House. On 11 March 1976, they finally took action. Ten armed police officers surrounded Kanit House. Gautier was believed to be out, so they waited for him to return. The light began to fade, a problem for the authorities because under Thai law the police can only enter a home between sunrise and sunset, unless they have a warrant. No one had arranged the paperwork for such a warrant. Then, just in time, Charles Sobhraj came home, with Monique and Ajay in tow. All three were arrested. Knippenberg was elated. He thought it was all over.

He was wrong.

'The Serpent' slithers away

The Thai police released their three suspects after being shown an American passport bearing the name of David Allen Gore, and the photograph of Charles Sobhraj. He had stolen it six weeks earlier in Hong Kong. The unflappable killer claimed Alain Gautier was away on business, and the information the Thai police had received was probably supplied by a jealous rival. The visa stamps in the passport of 'David Allen Gore' proved he was not in Thailand at the time of the Dutch couple's murder. Everything found in the flat was effortlessly explained away by the charming and professional schoolteacher from Iowa, 'David Gore'.

Knippenberg was furious, and contacted Ralph Nider at the US embassy to see if he could do anything about Sobhraj, as he was now using a stolen US passport. The call proved crucial because Nider was investigating the disappearance of a US citizen in Bangkok, Teresa Knowlton, whose bikini-clad body remained unidentified by Thai police. The two of them arranged their own visit to 504 Kanit House, where they seized dozens of bags of papers and the personal belongings of the young travellers who had stayed there and subsequently disappeared. The artefacts recovered included Cornelia's handbag, Henk's postal cheques, and a book on meditation inscribed by Teresa Knowlton. They leaked the story to the *Bangkok Post*, which posted it under the headline 'Web of Death' on 7 May, and included photographs of the known victims.

As planned, the Thai police were suddenly placed under immense pressure to find the killer. They looked again at the earlier death of Teresa Knowlton, and concluded from

Charles Sobhraj

the sand and the water in her lungs that her head had been held under the water. Her death was no accident, but a cold-blooded murder, and one probably linked to the murder of Stephanie Parry. Stephanie was wearing a mauve floral summer dress over red bikini bottoms when she was found; Teresa a floral bikini. The American press referred to the killings as 'The Bikini Murders', and the name stuck. The connection between Stephanie and Ved was soon established, linking another murder into the investigation.

Teresa Knowlton, it transpired, had stopped in Bangkok en route to the Kopan Tibetan monastery in Katmandu. She'd studied meditation in California looking for a new path after her drug-influenced teenage years in San Pedro and later Seattle. She'd thrived under the influence of Lama Yeshe, the monk who taught the course, taking him out on the ghost train at Disneyland and then agreeing to visit his monastery in return. But she wanted to visit Thailand, another Buddhist society, first. She checked into the Hotel Malaysia on Soi Ngarmduplee, where most Western tourists stayed. It was one of the few budget Thai hotels that had air-con, decent plumbing and a pool. There she ran into Ajay Chowdury, and he took her back to Kanit House to meet Charles Sobhraj, a self-professed Eastern mystic with a very different outlook on life from the lamas of Katmandu.

Sobhraj would later claim that Teresa, like Stephanie, was a drug courier. There's no evidence of this, though her friends back in Seattle did notice that money seemed to appear mysteriously in her account. Henk and Cornelia were quiet and studious, the former posting corrections to his chemistry PhD papers home to Amsterdam University as he travelled. The only thing the young travellers had in common with the drug-dealer Ved Hakim and the other victims was the misfortune to run into Charles Sobhraj.

At the same time that Teresa's body was exhumed, the body of Ved Hakim was, too. As the Thai authorities took the charred body out from the sheet of plastic in which it had been wrapped, its head fell off. His father Leon left the country in disgust and despair, having identified Ved, six months after the brutal murder. Despite compelling evidence implicating Charles Sobhraj in Thailand's crime wave, it seemed that Ved's killer would never be caught. The police had let him go, and by now with all his fake passports he could be anywhere in the world.

In fact, he was in Delhi, the capital of India. By now he was calling himself Daniel, and he was planning his most audacious crime yet.

The India crimes
Back in 1971, Sobhraj had attempted to rob a jewellery store in the Hotel Ashoka in Delhi, but had had to dump his loot at the airport after it was sealed off by the police. He was finally caught in a stolen car in Bombay and imprisoned in Tihar Jail. But he faked the symptoms of appendicitis and after having his appendix needlessly removed he managed to escape from the local hospital. He persuaded his then-wife Chantal to drug his guard and then take his place in the bed whilst he fled. She never forgave him for her subsequent arrest and imprisonment.

Now Sobhraj believed he could pull off another jewel heist and this time get away with the stolen goods. His escape plan involved flying to South America and setting up a false identity there, and for this he needed passports for himself, Monique and his other partners in crime. An opportunity to obtain his favourite type of passports, French ones, presented itself when he met a group of French students who were on a tour of Asia. Sobhraj befriended them and plotted to drug them and steal their precious passports.

In the restaurant of the Vikram Hotel in Delhi, he handed the group of 60 or so students some pills, which he claimed would protect them from dysentery. The plan was for the students to become sleepy after their meal, at which point Sobhraj could quietly help himself to whatever they kept in their hotel rooms. But something went badly wrong. Sobhraj misjudged the dose of sedatives he gave them, or perhaps failed to take account of the reaction the pills could cause when mixed with alcohol; whichever, the students began to complain of dizziness, and several of them collapsed whilst still in the hotel lobby. A doctor was called, and then the police, and then the French consul. With so many victims all in the same place and at the same time, even Sobhraj could not keep control of the situation. One of the policemen who arrived at the scene was Superintendent Tuli, one of the few Indian policemen who knew Sobhraj from his prior crimes in India: he identified 'Daniel' as the international fugitive Charles Sobhraj thanks to the scar left by his appendix operation. He was promptly arrested on suspicion of murder.

There were other crimes that the police did not yet know of: the death of French traveller Luke Soloman, who had died of a drug overdose after meeting Charles Sobhraj in Delhi a few days before the Vikram Hotel debacle, and the death of Israeli tourist Alan Aaron Jacobs, found dead in his bed in a hotel room in the holy Indian city of Varanasi. Sobhraj would later tell the writer Richard Neville that Jacobs was the only victim he ever felt sorry for, as he was a hard-working crane driver whom Sobhraj killed by accident: all Sobhraj wanted was his Israeli passport. At his trial Sobhraj would be charged with these killings, too – although not with another case to which he was linked, that of a taxi-driver called Mohammad Habib, who disappeared whilst driving Sobhraj around in Pakistan in 1972; nor with the death of middle-aged Frenchman Andre Breugnot, whose death in a bathtub in Chiangmai was ruled an accident, but which Charles later claimed was the result of his handiwork.

'The Serpent' on trial

On 5 July 1977, a year after his arrest, Charles Sobhraj was led into Old Delhi's Tishasari courthouse to stand trial. He claimed that his extraordinary life of crime had been 'a protest against the French legal system', which he complained had stolen his youth. It was presumably a reference to the time he spent in Poissy prison in Paris back in 1963, after being convicted of burglary at the age of 19. He served three years, and then in 1969 did a further eight months, this time for car theft. His antagonism to France, and to the West in general, stemmed from his upbringing in Saigon, South Vietnam – a war-torn French colony when Charles was born there in 1944. He never knew his natural father, an Indian moneylender, and was brought up by his mother, an illiterate Vietnamese woman. She met a French lieutenant named Alphonse Darreau, who helped raise Charles but refused to bestow upon him the Darreau family name. When they left Vietnam for France, Charles always felt like an outsider, unwanted by either his family or the country in which he was brought up. Crime, he now claimed, was his revenge against this perceived injustice.

He gave interviews to Richard Neville whilst the trial progressed and, according to Neville, Sobhraj confessed to five murders in Thailand and two in Nepal. His story was that he was employed by the Triads, the East's version of the Mafia, who ran a drug cartel from Hong Kong. All his victims, he claimed, were involved in drug trafficking. The killings were nothing personal, but just business. He later spoke at length to a second writer, Thomas Thompson, who used the interviews to write a best-selling book called *Serpentine*. By then Sobhraj was recanting all his confessions, however, and threatened to sue the publishers. For legal reasons, Thompson changed the names of many of the characters in his book, which explains why so many accounts of the case currently posted on the Internet call certain victims by incorrect names ('Jennie Bolliver' for Teresa Knowlton, 'Charmayne Carrou' for Stephanie Parry, 'Annabella Tremont' for Connie Jo Bronzich and 'Laddie DuParr' for Laurent Carrière).

But whilst bragging of his crimes to writers outside the court, on the witness stand Sobhraj maintained his total innocence of any involvement in the murders. The courts did not believe him. They heard how he cashed the traveller's cheques and stole the passport of the Israeli crane-driver Alan Aaron Jacobs. An Australian nurse called Mary Ellen Eather testified that she had been an accomplice in the poisoning of Luke Solomon's chicken curry, which subsequently proved fatal. Sobhraj was found guilty in both cases and sentenced to life imprisonment. He was also sentenced to two years for the drugging of the students at the Vikram Hotel. He could not be tried for the crimes in Thailand – he faced extradition when he had served his time in India. If convicted there, he would almost certainly face death by firing squad. Life in an Indian jail was highly preferable – particularly as Sobhraj had the money and charm to make his stay a relatively comfortable one.

'The Serpent' caged – and free

On Sunday 17 March 1986, Charles Sobhraj threw a birthday party in Tihar Jail in Delhi. Such gatherings were against the rules but the Sobhraj soirées were legendary and enjoyed by fellow-prisoners and staff alike. The prison warders were his guests of honour. They happily tucked into the fruit and sweets that had been smuggled in by two of Charles's ex-cell-mates. Moments later they were all unconscious, and Sobhraj was in a getaway car speeding through the crowded streets of the Indian capital. After ten years behind bars he was free once more.

Indeed, after years of court appeals, Sobhraj had succeeded in getting all of his convictions overturned by higher courts in India. The only cloud in his otherwise clear blue sky was the prospect of extradition to Thailand, and the possibility of facing a firing squad. In December 1985, the Indian High Court upheld a decision to allow his extradition to stand trial for the murders of Henk and Cordelia. It may have been this that prompted his decision to escape. When he was recaptured at the *O Coquiero* restaurant in the beach resort of Goa, on India's south-west coast, he was sentenced to a further ten years in jail for his escape. It would bring his total amount of time in the Indian prison system to 21 years – one year longer than the Thai statute of limitations.

That meant that when he was finally released from Tihar in 1997 he could not be tried for the murders he was alleged to have committed in Thailand. Instead, he was deported back to France. One of his first acts was to pray in front of the statue of St Teresa in Notre Dame Cathedral.

For the next seven years Sobhraj lived the celebrity lifestyle of a world-famous ex-convict, charging large sums of money in return for interviews and selling the movie rights to his life story. It seemed as though 'The Serpent' had, in the end, had the last laugh. But he then made what remains perhaps his most inexplicable move: he returned to the one country in the world that still had a valid arrest warrant for him, Nepal. There is no statute of limitations in Nepal, and Sobhraj was still wanted for the murders of Connie Jo Bronzich and Laurent Carrière. He was spotted in a casino in Kathmandu and arrested whilst in the middle of a game of baccarat. On 20 August 2004 he was found guilty of Connie Jo's murder and sentenced to life imprisonment. In September 2014 he was convicted of murdering Laurent Carrière and handed a second life-term.

After his release from prison in 1997, Sobhraj sued members of the press who called him a 'serial killer', pointing out that his earlier convictions had been overturned. His current convictions once again earn him the dubious distinction of that title, however. He is almost unique amongst his breed: his motivation was not one of sexual sadism. What, then, drove him to commit such heinous crimes? Money? He made a few thousand dollars from cashing his victims' traveller's cheques, but nothing truly substantial. He made more selling gems. Was he a travelling hit-man working for an organized crime gang, as he claimed? The travel journal of Henk and Cordelia appears to rule that out, but instead confirms they were innocent tourists. Most serial killers have a 'patch' in which they commit their crimes, returning to the safety of familiar ground time and again. Sobhraj, in contrast, left a trail of blood halfway around the world. He killed people of both sexes, the young and the middle-aged.

In the end, it begins to look, chillingly, as though he simply killed because he could. He appeared to want to teach the Western tourists who flocked East in search of spiritual enlightenment how naive they were, how easily manipulated, how stupidly trusting. He, who had from an early age had to fight for everything he got, resented the ease with which the privileged Westerners cast off their materialism in their quest for something 'deeper'. What could be deeper than life, and death – the power of which he soon realized he held in his hands?

'Be careful', he seemed to say to the travellers, 'or you might run into someone crazy, and dangerous, a person more depraved than you could even dream of.' And to prove his point, he became that person, that nightmare, that twisted, all-powerful god. Sobhraj became the first serial killer to operate on a truly global scale. In an ever-more closely connected world, he is unlikely to be the last.

Inexplicably, Sobhraj returned to Nepal in 2003 where he was arrested yet again and given a life-sentence for the 1975 murders of Bronzich and Carrière.

Index